Reaching Out

Reaching Out

*the guide
to writing a terrific
Dear Birthmother Letter*

Nelson Handel

Foreword by Carol LieberWilkins, M.A.

Marriage and Family Therapist, Adoption Counselor

**EasternEdge
Press**
Los Angeles
www.DearBirthmotherLetter.com

FIRST EDITION   October 2002

printed in U.S.A   *9 8 7 6 5 4 3 2 1*

ISBN 0-9716198-2-4

DEDICATION

This book is foremost dedicated to my wife, Elicia, without whose vast and unfathomable patience I would never, in this lifetime, have put to page word one. Despite all the words I have put there since, I have yet to discover any that fully encompass my love for her.

Coming in a close second is our son, Charlie, the journey to whom led directly to both this text, and the desire to help others achieve a small measure of the joy, love, sleepless nights, rollicking belly laughs, and endless wonder he has brought to our lives. That's him on the cover. Ain't he a lookah?

My sincere thanks to the many adoption professionals who lent their wisdom, guidance, and experience both to our adoption journey and to this book, especially Doug Donnelly, Esq., Carole LieberWilkins M.A., Jennifer Walker, L.C.S.W., Cindy Kent Lederer, L.C.S.W., and Mark Demaray, Esq. And thanks, too, to my editor, Patricia Saphier, for her gentle eye.

And lastly, to Charlie's birthmother, K, and all the birthmothers everywhere who, through strength, commitment, and uncommon love, see their children into the arms of caring families everywhere.

CONTENTS

FOREWORD

Beginning Your Adoption Journey
by
Carol LieberWilkins, M.A.
Marriage and Family Therapist, Adoption Counselor

It is my great honor to be asked to write the foreword to this book. As an adoption educator and psychotherapist specializing in infertility and family-building options since 1985, I've guided hundreds of couples (and singles) through the emotional mine fields of their adoption journey.

It will probably surprise you to learn that almost all prospective adoptive parents with whom I have worked have been absolutely certain they would never meet a birthmother or birthfather because they *(check all that apply to you)*:

- ❏ are too tall
- ❏ are too short
- ❏ are too skinny
- ❏ are too fat
- ❏ are too Jewish
- ❏ are too Christian
- ❏ are too Catholic
- ❏ are too Buddhist
- ❏ are a mixed faith couple, or not religious at all, or undecided
- ❏ are too old
- ❏ are too young
- ❏ are not educated enough, or too well educated
- ❏ are too wealthy (yes!)
- ❏ are not wealthy enough
- ❏ live in a huge house
- ❏ live in a modest apartment
- ❏ have curly hair
- ❏ have straight hair
- ❏ are single
- ❏ have tons of family locally
- ❏ have family living too far away
- ❏ all their family is dead
- ❏ live in the big city
- ❏ live in the suburbs
- ❏ live in the country
- ❏ are disabled
- ❏ are a minority
- ❏ are not a minority
- ❏ are infertility thrashed
- ❏ haven't done enough infertility treatment to be worthy
- ❏ already have one or two children
- ❏ have no children yet
- ❏ have already decided they are not worthy to become parents so why would they be chosen
- ❏ are too average
- ❏ are not average enough
- ❏ or…

Be honest, how many lines did you check?

Here's something else that will surprise you. Everyone that I have ever counseled who remained on the adoption path became a parent, despite having any or all of the perceived "deficits" above.

Coming to adoption after years of suffering from infertility usually leaves us pessimistic, frightened and intimidated. We feel "unentitled" to become parents. I can use the word "we" here because I, too, walked this path. I am a mother who became a mother through the magical, mystical, complex, complicated, often difficult, spiritual process of adoption.

It is common and normal for everyone approaching adoption to have fears, including that they will not be chosen. Many are afraid that an open adoption will result in complicated relationships with birthparents. Then there is THE BIG FEAR: the feeling of being threatened by birthparents.

The more you understand birthparents and the adoption process, however, the more you will realize how untrue are many of the myths surrounding open adoption, and how little you have to fear. Birthparents are as different in their needs, personalities, and styles as are prospective parents. For every personal aspect that you think will cast you in a negative light, there is a birthparent looking for someone exactly like you.

And most of them are at least as frightened as you are. They are often alone, confused, and in the most difficult situation any of us can possibly imagine. They cannot parent the child they have created and desperately need someone who can and will. They are often embarrassed, feel foolish, and feel "unentitled" just like you.

To the birthmother or birthfather, you look like you have it all. You (if not single) are married; you are old enough and mature enough to be good parents (as if that were a guarantee!!); in most cases you have more financial security than the birthparents (no matter how much you have); you want to parent; you have medical insurance, support systems, jobs, and each other; and more. In other words you have and are many of the things birthparents do not have and are not.

Being Who You Are

Over the years, I have guided many clients through the process of creating their dear birthmother letters. As strange as it may sound, one of the most difficult aspects has been to get them to be who they really are. Coming from that unentitled place, they feel they have to create a false image of themselves in order to be acceptable to a birthmother.

Too often, they have been guided to alter the details of their lives and the real essence of who they are. Someone told them to change their names ("Myrtle is a homely name, could you be Missy?"), or the spelling of their names ("Susan is so formal, but birth mothers can relate to Susie"), decrease the importance of things that are vital in their lives ("don't mention that you, as a woman, work"), or increase certain aspects that may be of little importance at all ("couldn't you be more outdoors-y?"). And prospective parents usually comply, out of fear of the unknown and the misinformed belief that these are the only ways to "get chosen."

When these lost souls and I finally speak, I encourage them as I now encourage you: above all else, be yourself and be true to yourself. Do you really want to start out a relationship with the person who will forever be connected to your family by shading the truth? Do you want later to speak with your kids about their adoption process knowing that you were "chosen" or matched based on untruths? And is it possible to truly know and trust a birthmother with whom you want to develop a relationship if you start out on false premises?

Untruths are hard to maintain. Masking yourself taints the process and the spirit of adoption.

Imagine instead, birthparents and adopting parents coming together to create a family. You perfectly meet each other's needs: the child will have a loving family, the birthmother will rest assured her child is safe, and you will finally be parents. Carry this positive image of the adoption triad in your mind as you embark on this wonderful journey, and you will be properly oriented to succeed.

This book teaches you concepts and approaches consistent with good mental health. It will show you how to be *congruent*, in other words, to have your outsides match your insides. It encourages you to trust, both yourself and the birthparent you hope to meet. And it will help you to introduce yourself to birthparents feeling very comfortable that the people described in your Dear Birthmother letter are absolutely you.

I hope this Guide fills you with confidence and enthusiasm as you begin the process of bringing into your lives the birthfamily that will eventually fulfill your dreams of parenthood. It's a wonderful journey, and one I urge you to honor and appreciate.

May your path be blessed with all the joys that adoption can bring.

Carole LieberWilkins, MA
Los Angeles, September 23, 2001

Reaching Out

INTRODUCTION

When my wife and I scrabbled together the first version of our Dear Birthmother letter, we sent it to our adoption attorney for comments, hoping that his twenty-plus years of experience in the field would yield some insight and guidance.

He called us almost immediately. He told us that, after all of his time in the adoption game, he almost *never* comments on other people's letters. Why? Because the letters he thinks are terrible sometimes work and the letters he loves sometimes do not. After being humbled by the unpredictability of human nature in both directions numerous times, he had simply thrown up his hands and given the whole matter a big shrug.

Why, you might ask yourself, would I tell this story in the first paragraph of a book purporting to help you write a terrific Dear Birthmother letter? To impress upon you the core philosophy of this text: *Have No Fear.*

No one can ever tell you for certain what will or will not affect another person, what fact or locution will be the hook that catches someone's interest, and I'm not about to start. My goal is to give you a context in which to consider the choices you will make when you create this very personal document. The key word here is *choices*. In the end, the letter you write and release to the world is yours and, whatever it turns out to be, it will reflect who you are. I cannot tell you what is right or wrong because there is no right or wrong when you're writing about your own life. There is only what you feel to be true, honest, and appropriate to the moment.

You may agree with some of the ideas I propose or you may not. My goal is to illuminate the various issues at play so you can make active, informed choices. My hope is that these insights, ideas, and suggestions assist you to express yourself authentically, directly, and from the heart.

You are at the beginning of your adoption journey. Many of the subjects you will address in this letter are still muddled with fear, ambiguity, and doubt (the three-headed Hydra that guards the gates of any new experience). This text will confront some of these issues as well.

The writing process itself can be joyous, difficult, soul-searching, trying, and fulfilling. But put your fears aside. Whatever comes out the other end will be terrific and almost certainly help you to the family you so lovingly desire.

Some Notes About the Book

Dear Birthmother letters go by a number of names, including family resume, letter of introduction, personal profile, parent profile, and family presentation. For the purpose of this text, we will agree to call them all Dear Birthmother letters. Some are brief one-page affairs, others forty-page "life books" full of pictures and supporting documents. Whatever the name, and whatever physical form they take, the goal remains the same: to introduce you to birthmothers looking to find parents for their children.

This guide is a result of discussions with adoption attorneys, adoption social workers, agency professionals, mental healthcare professionals specializing in adoption and infertility issues, and other specialists. It also draws heavily on my own personal experience as a journalist, an essayist, and an adoptive parent. I'll do my best to be objective and to present all sides of issues on which wise people sometimes disagree.

It's the privilege of an author to spout off on issues of personal consequence, and I will occasionally subject you to my biased opinion on such matters. I'll do my best to be up front about it, so that it's clear when I'm speaking subjectively. My biases should become obvious as you read this book, but if you'd like to learn more about them now, please see the essay, "Love for Sale," included here on page 135, reprinted from Adoptive Families Magazine. It details the struggles my wife and I had when we sat down to write our letter. You may see a bit of yourself in our story.

How-to books can be dreadfully dull, so please excuse me in advance if I do my best to make this guide both useful and readable. I'll try not to flap my gums excessively, but occasionally, flap I will.

Throughout the text, I employ examples from actual Dear Birthmother letters to illustrate the points being discussed, often with a small note pointing out the strengths and weaknesses of a particular bit of writing. The appendixes include the full text of a number of letters, including our own. Reading these samples should give you an overall sense of how the process can work.

I use the term "birthmother" throughout the text to include all birthparents. Birthfathers, the often forgotten members of the adoption triad, can play a significant role in the formulation of the final adoption plan. I've made this choice more for grammatical ease—to avoid all those "his or her" type locutions—than with an editorial intention to exclude anyone.

Keep in mind also that a birthmother is not a birthmother until she has completed the placement of her child, and many resent being called so before it is appropriate. Until then, she is an *expectant mother* and should be considered as such. Again, I beg your nomenclatural indulgence.

Likewise, I address all potential adoptive parents as married couples, not because there aren't single or same-sex-couple adopters, but because to constantly acknowledge them would lead to similarly wordy and complex prose. If you are a single person or same-sex couple seeking to adopt, please feel as included in this text as anyone else. Plans for future editions include sections addressing the special circumstances of these types of adoptions.

This book is primarily concerned with the letter of introduction that begins an open adoption. Hence, for the purpose of this text, I define an *open adoption* as one in which the birthparents choose the adoptive parents for their child, and the adoptive parents, in turn, choose the birthparents of theirs. All other forms of "openness" in adoption are matters for discussion between you, your adoption professional, and your birthmother at the appropriate time.

The three-leaf graphic you see throughout the book represents for me the three lives in the adoption triad—adoptive parents, birthparents, and child—all growing, green and healthy, from the same branch of the tree of life.

No Cookies Cut Here

It's not the intention of this book to make all Dear Birthmother letters sound alike. Quite the opposite. Every letter should be unique, individual, and personal. This guide hopes to provide tips, strategies, and ideas to help you express yourself better, not a cookie cutter mold into which you must fit. Think of this as a tool kit for the process of communication.

However, some adoption professionals will give you very specific instructions as to what to include or exclude from your Dear Birthmother letter. Since most of them are highly qualified and know well the types of birthmothers whom they attract (and since you are paying good money for their expertise), I advise you to take full advantage of their suggestions. This book is intended to augment and compliment their advice, not supercede it.

Writing Begins with Rewriting

Why is this tip, here, so early in the book? Because most people view rewriting with the same disdain as they view dead rodents: a thing they wish the care of to someone else. Here's a secret of the writing trade: professional writers love to rewrite. Why? **Anticipating a rewrite allows you to write more freely.**

The most common cause of literary brain freeze is the pressure to make everything perfect the first time you put it on the page. People spend hours laboring over a single sentence, unable to continue until it's crystalline. When you're writing intimately about yourself, it's even more difficult. With each word on the page, all those self-critical voices start screaming in your head: *What will they think of me? What if they misunderstand? I can't say that, it's too em-*

barrassing! It's enough to reduce grown men and women to tears (ask my wife). With all that noise going on, it's no wonder you're having trouble getting anything done.

So, relax.

Writing a Dear Birthmother letter is not the most difficult thing in the world, it only seems that way. A good Dear Birthmother letter is created systematically, paragraph by paragraph, and then assembled and edited into a cohesive whole. Knowing this should allow you to write freely and not worry about confusion, redundancy, imperfection, or inappropriateness. When you write, write whatever comes into your head. Just get it down on the page. You can always (and probably will) change it later.

A Personal Word about Surviving the Journey to Adoption

My wife and I discovered early on in our adoption journey that, like infertility (IF), the adoption process asks you to surrender a great degree of control over the outcome. This is often very difficult for high-functioning, modern people who believe they can affect direct change to their lives. Adoption and infertility teach you that sometimes, you can't.

This is not to say that you are powerless. The wonderful thing about adoption, as opposed to IF, is that if you keep at it, you will have a child. The difficult thing is that, like IF, you never know precisely which action will bring it about. You could run as fast as you can down one road, only to find yourself exhausted, spent, and at a dead end. In the next eyelash flutter, a child could enter your life from the least expected direction.

We maintained our sanity by doing things to keep moving forward, even if we didn't always know where forward was. Calm, steady perseverance was the key, staying within ourselves as best we could, but also keeping our energy steadily flowing out into the universe in a progression of different ways. We tried not to put too much hope in any single action and trusted that, collectively, the sum of all our actions would lead us to our goal. And it did.

This is a rather long way of saying that, in choosing to read this book, you've taken a positive step on your journey. For many readers, it will be your first step. For others, who may be revisiting their letter in the hopes of improving it, it's just another step along the road to family. In either case, I hope the experience will be educational, generative, and have value in and of itself.

And, of course, my ultimate hope is that you should soon see your child, the one that you are meant to parent, cradled in your loving arms.

THE GOLDEN RULES

Yes, just a page or two after I said there was no right or wrong to writing a Dear Birthmother letter, I'm going to lay a few rules on you. Perhaps "rules" is a bad word to describe this chapter; these philosophies represent the core values upon which this book is based. Taken as a whole, they provide a great mind set with which to begin not just your letter writing, but your whole adoption journey as well.

#1 - The Goal of a Dear Birthmother Letter is to Connect with the Birthmother Who is Right for You.

Adoption professionals all agree that successful open adoptions—where the right baby makes it into the right home—occur when potential adoptive parents and birthmothers make a strong personal connection prior to the birth of the child. So, this first Golden Rule contains two bits of essential wisdom.

First, you must understand that your goal is to connect with a *birthmother*, not a child. If you are looking to adopt a newborn, you can't pick your child; you can only pick your child's birthmother. After all this time hoping for a baby, suddenly you must hope for an adult, and that's a change in consciousness. To find the baby that's meant to be a part of your family, you must connect with the birthmother who is right for you.

And there's that phrase again: *who is right for you.*

Not every birthmother will match up well with every potential adoptive parent. Personal temperaments, life philosophies, and personalities vary, ways of communicating differ, and personal rhythms sometimes don't click. The same variables that govern all interpersonal communication are naturally at play, and often amplified, within the high-stakes context of a birthmother/potential adoptive parent relationship.

A successful open adoption grows from a certain natural comfort level between the participants, a sense of ease that is reassuring to both parties. Your birthmother needn't be "just like you," either. This type of simpatico can easily exist between people of widely differing backgrounds and experience. When you finally meet the birthmother who's right for you, it may surprise you to find that you come from very different places yet share much common ground.

The best way to heighten your chances of meeting that special someone is to present an accurate and insightful impression of yourselves in your Dear Birthmother letter. The more authentically your letter communicates the essence of who you are, the better chance you have of connecting with the birthmother who shares those feelings.

#2 - Whatever It Is, It's You

Too many potential adoptive parents get tied up trying to perfect this letter and to control how every birthmother will respond to it. This goal is unattainable. It simply leads to countless drafts torn up in frustration, and ultimately, to disappointing results.

So it bears repeating: **Whatever it is, it's you.**

What you say, the order in which you say it, what you omit, the language you use–whatever form this letter takes when you finally release it to the world–will reveal all sorts of things about you that you can't anticipate. On some level, therein lies its special power.

So while it is obviously extremely important that you give this letter your fullest attention, care, and love, you also need keep a clear perspective about what you are trying to accomplish. It's almost impossible to predict what readers will think, especially with such personal material. Let it go. Trust yourself. It will be a picture of you.

#3 - Don't Judge Yourself Too Harshly

To the writer, a Dear Birthmother letter can be a little like the picture of Dorian Gray, reflecting back at you all of your imperfections. Harsh judgement becomes especially tempting when you start to compare your life to the lives in other people's letters. It's easy to fall into the adoption version of "keeping up with the Joneses."

You may get upset because you're not a stay-at-home-mom, or because you are and don't have a career. You may feel you're not as wealthy as another couple, or that your neighborhood isn't as idyllic, or that you have strong religious beliefs, or that you don't.

In the words of the great philosophers: *balderdash and poppy-*

cock. Most of those insecurities stem from stereotypes of what a "perfect" family is, and it's all crap (pardon my French). **A perfect family is one full of love, support, and a dedication to raising a child as best it can.**

You can never predict how another person will look at you. For every birthmother who wants to place her child with a stay-at-home mother, there's one who thinks women who don't work are spoiled. For every birthmother who thinks the suburbs are wonderful, another can't imagine her child anywhere except the big city. For every one that loves houses, another likes apartments. And on and on.

The simple fact is that no one judges you as harshly as you judge yourself. In this case, no one is really judging you at all. Birthmothers are looking for something with which they can connect, some intangible that will make them want to pick up the phone and find out more about you. Sometimes it's the silliest things– your haircut (or lack of one), a bad joke you make, that your name is Sybil, that you like horses–and sometimes it's a deeply held core belief. It could be anything, and the only thing for sure is that no one knows for sure. So put your best face forward and be proud of who you are.

#4 - Be Yourself

The temptation, when you're first starting to write, is to think in mercantile terms, to think of yourself as a product to be packaged and sold. This is a natural instinct given our consumer culture and the number of advertising messages we absorb everyday. Many potential adoptive families find the whole Dear Birthmother letter process so distasteful that they choose to abandon the course of adoption altogether. They are either discouraged by what they feel is a need to present picture perfect, "Ken and Barbie" images of themselves, or they are turned off by the feeling that they are advertising for a baby.

My wife and I certainly wrestled with these issues. I wrote about them for *Offspring* and *Adoptive Families* magazines *[See Appendix 1: Love for Sale]*. And indeed, in some sense, writing a Dear Birthmother letter is constructing an image for yourself, an image you hope will appeal to a birthmother.

But primarily, a Dear Birthmother letter is an introduction, the purpose of which is to meet a person who may need your help (as you might need hers). You are not writing to persuade, as a sales pitch might do. **You are writing to open widely the door to your life and let a birthmother have a good peek inside.** Maybe even put out the welcome mat. The closer to your heart you can keep this thought, the freer of competitive concerns you will feel.

If you can't fully separate yourself from the feeling that you are selling something—and it would be disingenuous of me to suggest that you would be alone in this—at least sell yourself honestly. Don't pretend you're chicken if in fact you are steak. Always remember that your goal is to appeal not to just *any* birthmother, but rather to the one with whom you are likely to be able to form a strong connection.

Most importantly, don't begin this most important of life journeys with a lie, no matter how small it is. Now, more than ever, to thine own self be true.

#5 - Birthmothers Are Just Like You

At this point, early in your adoption journey, you probably still have preconceptions about who is the "typical" birthmother. Hopefully, you will encounter many sources that will disabuse you of your false impressions. Let me add my voice to the mix.

Common stereotypes of birthmothers include teen mothers, women with substance abuse issues, women with poor education, with no money, who are homeless, or have a host of other challenges. While some birthmothers do display some of these attributes, most of these stereotypes are dead wrong. For instance, studies show that unwed teens overwhelmingly choose to parent their children; the average birthmother is in her mid-20s.

Here's the secret that isn't a secret to anyone who speaks with a lot of birthmothers: birthparents are just like you, except with unplanned pregnancies to manage. They could be well-educated, or street smart, or not. They could live in wealthy homes, suburban apartments, or on a friend's floor. They could be married, or not, have other children, or not, etc…etc…etc.

Get whatever preconceptions you might have about them out of your mind. First, there are no "typical" birthmothers; each is individual and unique, just like you are. Almost anyone can have an unwanted pregnancy and choose to make an adoption plan, including (in no particular order): college students who aren't ready to parent, parents with children who feel they can't support another child, single professionals who want their child to have a father, women whose seemingly stable relationships break up mid-pregnancy, single women with fundamentalist Christian beliefs (or no religious beliefs at all), women who are fleeing domestic violence situations, women whose plan for the future doesn't include children, and on and on.

If birthmothers can be said to have anything in common, it is that they are givers. For the most part, they are generous, warm-hearted women who want the best for their children but don't feel able to provide it.

Why is this important to keep in mind when writing your Dear Birthmother letter? Because you must avoid making negative assumptions, (often based on these incorrect stereotypes) about who's reading your letter. Bad assumptions will cause you either to write in misplaced fear of birthmothers, or to second-guess yourself and try to be someone that you are not.

To connect with the right birthmother for you, it's essential that you express yourself as authentically as possible and have confidence that what you say is falling on open, compassionate ears–just like yours.

#6 - Respect your Birthmother

As you set out to write your Dear Birthmother letter, you must start to think about *to whom* you are writing. It's impossible to write to the Void. In order to write truly and compassionately, without condescension or pretense, you must form an image in your mind of your eventual birthmother. She should be someone you care about, someone with whom you can be vulnerable, and above all, someone you respect.

Birthmothers do have something in common. They are all walking down a road that is lined with shadows of emotional peril. It leads to one of the most personal and difficult choices a woman can make: placing her child into someone else's care. By understanding this simple fact, you can begin, with your letter, to light her way, to show her that traveling that road *with you* will be a safe, supportive, and respectful journey.

Another essential way to demonstrate respect for your birthmother, and all birthmothers, is to provide enough information to help them make the beginning of an informed decision. Providing as much salient information as you can will begin your relationship in an atmosphere of openness and equality. Information and respect are empowering, and the more confident a birthmother is with her choice of parents for her child, the less likely she is to change her mind later.

This is not a position embraced by all adoption professionals, however. Some advocate writing very short letters that provide little but the sketchiest information about you. This philosophy comes from a belief that too much information is confusing. One lawyer I spoke with, a former president of the Academy of California Adoption Lawyers and a proponent of informative Dear Birthmother letters, summed it up eloquently:

> *Keep in mind that a couple of very well respected adoption attorneys have told me that my way of doing resumes is nuts. They contend it gives the birthmother too much information. I respectfully disagree. I think you need to give her as much information as possible to assist her in making one of the biggest decisions of her life. In effect, I try to treat the birth mother the way I would want to be treated if I were in her shoes. I know that the application of the golden rule to adoption sounds bizarre, particularly when its proponent is an attorney, but my experience has demonstrated that it works. Birthmothers like to be treated with respect, and deserve that respect. The more common practice of giving just a little bit of information is an insult to her intelligence, and in many cases prevents her from making a choice that really promotes her peace of mind.*

Someday, your child will turn to you and ask about his or her birthmother. When s/he does, you will want to be able to answer from the fullness of your heart. You'll only be able to do that if their birthmother is someone you respect. Begin now.

#7 - Assume the Best

Most potential adoptive parents bring to the table the common misconception that making an adoption plan is a painful, torturous decision for a birthmother. This assumption likely stems from the fact that most have tried so hard to have children that the idea of placing one for adoption is impossible to imagine.

It is unwise to assume too much in your letter about how a birthmother is feeling. While certainly the process of placing a child is an emotional one, often that emotion is joy and relief that the child will have a happy and loving home. Birthmothers who are most likely to complete a placement are the ones who love their child and want the best for them. They see adoption as a positive step toward that goal.

For some birthmothers, the journey is very difficult, and for all, it is followed by a period of grieving. But by projecting in your letter one state or another, you run the risk of alienating someone who feels differently than you assume.

Assume the best. Be open, respectful, and sympathetic. You will give greater comfort to a birthmother by speaking of adoption as a blessing to all involved than by suggesting that it's a tragedy.

#8 - Be Positive

For couples who come to embrace adoption after infertility, it's common for all thoughts of starting a family to come with a measured dose of sorrow. Coming to terms with the inability to conceive involves a process of acceptance, grieving and healing. For many at this early stage of the adoption process, these sorrows are still fresh and the wounds raw.

These are natural and normal feelings, and need to be dealt with and processed as you move on in your journey towards family. But your Dear Birthmother letter is not the place to do it. Your letter is your opportunity to reach out in love and joy to the birthmother of your child.

Articulate the positive things you have to offer. State your case honestly, simply, and directly. It's not a bad thing to mention your infertility, or any other sorrow or difficulty that seems central to your life, but do so within the context of the positive things that adversity has taught you.

Don't waste time qualifying, equivocating over, or pointing out the deficiencies of your life. We all wish our homes were bigger, our incomes larger, or our relationship with our parents better, but compared to Birthmother Problem #1, most potential adoptive parents have it pretty good.

Put your best foot forward. Speak of adoption as an exciting process that will lead to happiness for all involved. Communicate the same positive messages to your birthmother that you hope one day to communicate to your child.

#9 - Be the Solution

This is the best tip for almost all your dealings with birthfamilies. Whether you are speaking on the phone, writing a letter, or meeting in person, endeavor to figure out what your birthmother needs most at that moment, and address yourself to that need to the best of your ability. This doesn't mean kowtow or pander to them—you must remain true to yourself—but you will inspire trust by caring for and addressing their issues.

Begin by understanding where most birthmothers are coming from. Their major concern, at least in the beginning of the process, is this HUGE problem they have to solve, their unplanned pregnancy. And, again for the most part, from their point of view, you have the skills or advantages that can help them solve it. Your Dear Birthmother letter is your first opportunity to demonstrate that.

By the time they are actively searching for a family, many birthmothers are already committed to making an adoption plan. Their central fear is that they will be unable to find the right family for their baby. Some are afraid that they won't know how to choose from among all the potential parents. A couple that projects a loving, "problem solving" attitude helps to alleviate these fears.

Address the issues important to a birthmother's decision-making process. Help them imagine you as the solution that they seek.

#10 - There is No Magic Formula...

...or secret map that will help you to find the perfect birthmother. The path is paved with common sense, generosity of spirit, and love. The clearer the picture you paint of your life, the more concretely a birthmother will be able to imagine who you are.

You cannot craft, shape, or otherwise control your letter to appeal to a certain type of person, you can only reveal yourself and trust that a certain type of person will respond to your story. The more authentic and heartfelt your communication, the better chance you have of connecting with the birthmother who is right for you.

THE GOLDEN RULES

(Post this over your desk as you work)

➢ The Goal of a Dear Birthmother Letter is to Connect with the Birthmother Who Is Right for You.

➢ Whatever it is, It's You.

➢ Don't Judge Yourself Too Harshly.

➢ Be Yourself.

➢ Birthmothers are Just Like You.

➢ Respect Your Birthmother.

➢ Assume the Best.

➢ Be Positive.

➢ Be the Solution.

➢ There is No Magic Formula...

THE LANGUAGE OF ADOPTION

Personally, I'm not a big fan of the extremes to which some people go to employ politically correct speech. **But language, to a growing mind, is a powerful thing, and the language in which you clothe adoption is the language of your child's self-esteem.** For this reason, it's imperative that you adopt positive adoption language before you adopt a child. If you don't use it already, now is the time to begin.

Here are some common terms to use when talking about the adoption process, along with phrases to avoid.

Negative Adoption Language	**Positive Adoption Language**
Real mother, natural mother	Birthmother, biological mother, genetic mother
Real father, natural father, "sperm donor"	Birthfather, biological father, genetic father

Negative Adoption Language	Positive Adoption Language
Give away, give up, put up for adoption	Place for adoption, choose adoption, make an adoption plan
She kept her baby	She chose to parent her baby
Fake mother, foster mother*	Adoptive mother, mother, mother by adoption (same for fathers)
A child of their own, their real child	Their biological child, child by birth, birthchild
Foreign adoption	International adoption, inter-country adoption
Mixed race child, mulatto	Biracial child, multiracial child
Handicapped child, disabled child	Child with special needs

*"Foster Mother/Father" are appropriate terms when used to describe a person who is providing temporary care to a child. They are inaccurate and disparaging when used to describe adoptive parents.

STYLE

All terrific Dear Birthmother letters, no matter what their final form, share certain common traits that make them appropriate, appealing, lively, and affective. Here are some guidelines to proper style.

Use Direct Address

Good Dear Birthmother letters talk *to* someone, a birthmother, directly. Just like a personal letter, employ the second person pronoun "you" to make your letter immediate and personal.

➢ **Begin with salutary opening:**

Dear Special Person, Dear friend, To a brave young woman, Dearest one, In love we write you, Welcome to our hearts, Hello, etc.

> ### End with a dedicated close:

Yours truly, Sincerely, With love, With hugs, Holding you close from afar, From our heart...

A brief note here about the use of the term "birthmother." Though everyone in the adoption triad calls this letter what it is, a Dear Birthmother letter, the fact remains that birthmothers are not actually birthmothers until they complete the placement of their child. Despite their acknowledgment of the term, many birthmoms dislike being called so prior to placement, and there is certainly no reason to do so within your introductory letter. To be safe, avoid the term until it is appropriate. Before then, use the term *expectant mother.*

Length

Adoption professionals disagree as to the proper length for a Dear Birthmother letter. Some advocate a one-page document with a single picture while others want extravagant, handmade arts-and-crafts projects; some suggest two-to-three pages with a photo montage, and still others, forty-page "life books." No matter how brief or lengthy your letter, it will seem longer if it's badly written.

17th century French mathematician and writer Blaise Pascal once famously ended a correspondence with the line, "I have only made this letter longer because I have not had the time to make it shorter." A good letter says what it needs to say, comprehensively, without becoming tedious. Strunk & White in *The Elements of Style* remind us "that when a sentence is made stronger, it usually becomes shorter. Thus brevity is a by-product of vigor."

Vigorous writing also reads more easily than weak writing. A longer letter written in a breezy and easy-to-read voice may seem shorter than a brief letter written in a dense, scholarly tone. Style and voice play an important role in how a reader experiences length. This book is good example. It takes 130 pages or so to describe a short letter. But it's written in a familiar and casual voice that (hopefully) makes it feel like a quick and enjoyable read.

When it comes to length, take these three points as guidance:

➢ **Make sure your letter expresses your views fully, but is as compact and essential as possible.** Edit vigorously. Avoid redundancy. Limit unnecessary chatter. Make every verb work and every anecdote reveal.

➢ If your adoption professional strongly advocates letters of a certain length, **give his or her recommendation serious consideration.** But remember, in the end, these people work for you. Feel free to politely disagree if you wish. You need to feel comfortable and well represented by your letter.

➢ **Note the length of the other letters with which yours will be reviewed.** If your adoption professional presents birthmothers with just two or three letters to choose from, yours can afford to be slightly longer. If birthmothers are being asked to review twenty letters, a letter that's twice the length of all the rest might turn them off. Then again, it may not. Be comfortable with how you fit into the mix.

Employ Subheads

A gray page, one full of nothing but type, is off-putting to look at and inherently difficult to read. Photos will help break up the text, but text elements can also help organize the reader's experience and make it more enjoyable.

Subheads, those smaller headlines you often see in magazine articles, provide a terrific opportunity to break up the text while simultaneously cluing in your readers about what's to come. This chapter has used three subheads already: *Use direct address, Length,* and *Employ Subheads.*

A reader will often scan the subheads of a page before reading it, even if only unconsciously, especially in a document that is essentially informational. You might have done that before you began this chapter. Subheads also help readers to follow the flow of ideas.

Format your subheads with an alternative type style, either **Bold,** *Bold Italic,* **Slightly Larger Type**, or 𝔄 𝒟𝒾𝒻𝒻𝑒𝓇𝑒𝓃𝓉 𝒯𝓎𝓅𝑒𝒻𝒶𝒸𝑒 𝓔𝓷𝓽𝓲𝓻𝓮𝓵𝔂. Using simple typographical variation helps refresh the eye and "reset the brain" between sections (as can a little bit of white page–the space between paragraphs).

Subheads can be as formal or as informal as you wish, but keep them consistent with the tone of the rest of your letter. Creative or unusual subheads often catch a reader's interest effectively, so feel free to spice it up if the mood strikes you.

> ➤ **Here's a good example of one couple who had some fun with their subheads:**

Welcome to our garden!

The seeds are planted (a little background)

Sunshine in our garden (getting married and ready for kids)

Tending the family garden (why we want to adopt)

Wanna grow our gardens together?

Anything that makes your letter seem friendlier, lighter, and more accessible is a very good thing. Humor is good, but don't work too hard to be funny. Let your humor be gentle and natural. As you read the full-length samples in the back of the book, note how the use of subheads gives each a different tone and character.

Write Short Paragraphs

Another great way to make a long manuscript more appealing to the eye (and easier to digest) is to keep your paragraphs brief. Long paragraphs tend to look imposing, while shorter paragraphs help give the reader a feeling of speed and liveliness. Limit your paragraphs to three or four sentences if you can. Short paragraphs break up your thoughts into easily digestible, bite-size chunks.

On this and the next page are two examples of the same text (the introductory information from the last section). The first example contains the text in a single paragraph. The second divides it into shorter paragraphs.

First, glance at the two examples objectively, without reading them. Does one seem more inviting?

Now read them, and see which is more informative to you.

➢ **Example #1**

A gray page, one full of type, is inherently difficult to read and off-putting to view. Photos will help break up the text, but text elements also help organize the reader's experience and make it more enjoyable. Subheads, those smaller headlines you often see in magazine articles, provide a terrific opportunity to break up the text while simultaneously cluing in your readers to what's next. This chapter has used three subheads already: Use Direct Address, Length, *and* Employ Subheads. *A reader will often scan the subheads of a page before reading it, even if only unconsciously, especially in a document that is essentially informative. You might have done that before you began this chapter. Subheads also help readers follow the text's flow of ideas. Format your subheads with an alternate type style, either* **Bold,** ***Bold Italic,*** Slightly Larger Type, *or* 𝒜 𝒟ifferent 𝒯ypeface 𝓔ntirely. *Using simple typographical variation helps refresh the eye and "reset the brain" between sections.*

➤ **Example #2**

A gray page, one full of type, is inherently difficult to read and off-putting to view. Photos will help break up the text, but text elements also help organize the reader's experience and make it more enjoyable.

Subheads, those smaller headlines you often see in magazine articles, provide a terrific opportunity to break up the text while simultaneously cluing in your readers to what's next. This chapter has used three subheads already: Use Direct Address, Length, *and* Employ Subheads.

A reader will often scan the subheads of a page before reading it, even if only unconsciously, especially in a document that is essentially informative. You might have done that before you began this chapter. Subheads also help readers follow the text's flow of ideas.

Format your subheads with an alternate type style, either **Bold,** ***Bold Italic,*** Slightly Larger Type, *or* 𝒜 𝒟ifferent 𝒯ypeface 𝓔ntirely. *Using simple typographical variation helps refresh the eye and "reset the brain" between sections.*

Check your letter for long paragraphs and divide up any that seem like big blocks of gray. Begin a new paragraph whenever you begin a new idea. Without changing your content, your reader will more readily get the message.

Don't Oversell

Have you ever met someone at a party who, within 15 minutes, tells you their entire life story, complete with myriad details about people you don't know and places you haven't been? There's such a thing as *too* much information. A good Dear Birthmother letter is an introduction to your life, not an autobiography. It should give the reader a flavor of your views and feelings on each of its subject areas, without going too deeply into minutia.

To a birthmother, you're a little like that person at the party. The room is crowded, she's just met you, and she has no context in which to appreciate your story. You want to tell her just enough to want, say, to have a cup of herbal tea with you the next day (she's pregnant, so no coffee), and not so much that she starts looking around the room to find someone who's not so wearisome.

Save something for later. For now, stick to a few big ideas and illustrate them with specificity. Your goal is to pique her interest and make her comfortable enough to want to get to know you better.

Keep Sections Short and To the Point

When you are writing a section, resist straying off topic. Sure, everything in your life is connected to everything else, but stay as "on message" as you can. You'll make it easier for your reader to follow your story and to build a cogent picture of who you are.

Let Your Ideas Flow

The phrase "flow of ideas" describes the way each part of a written document sets up the next and builds upon the last. Ideas should progress in a way that brings you deeper into the subject as you read. Keep this in mind when you are assembling your final drafts.

Use a Consistent Voice

No matter who writes it, your Dear Birthmother letter should appear to come from both of you (if you are a couple). This avoids giving a birthmother the impression that one of you is disinterested.

Always use "we" as the base speaking voice of the letter. If you choose to include sections written by just one of you, make sure that you clearly indicate who is the "I" with the use of a subhead or other device. I urge you to do so *before* the voice changes. There's nothing more confusing than when we shift our speaking voices in the middle of a paragraph without an explanation, as if suddenly there are two of us speaking.

See what I mean?

A brief word here concerning writing about yourself in the third person ("she, he, they"). Unless it is within the context of a first-person narrative, it tends to distance the reader from what is being described. Here's an example:

> ## First Person

The minute I met Sylvia, I knew she was bright, warmhearted, and had a great way with people. Everyone seemed to like her, and when she walked into the room, it just lit up.

> ## Third Person

Sylvia is a warm person. She likes to sail and play golf, just like John does. John is a nice guy and everyone likes him. Together, they lead a very active lifestyle, full of fun.

Using the third person begs the question, "who is talking to me?" Though many letters use this so-called "reporter's" voice, I think they do it more for grammatical convenience than conscious affect. It's much stronger to choose a form that employs first person narrative.

If you do choose to use the reporter's voice, make sure to balance it with lots of specific, personal stories to which a reader can really relate. Dear Birthmother letters work best when they are personal and direct.

Don't "It" the Baby

The exception to the above rule is when you are referring to the unborn child that you hope to adopt. ALWAYS use a third person personal pronoun: *he, she, him, her, his, hers, s/he,* or *his or her.* NEVER refer to the baby as "it." He or she is a person, not a rug, and some birthmothers will be turned off by the impersonal quality of Baby It.

Though using the phrase *his or her* can be awkward, it's best to use it and stay gender neutral. The exception, of course, is if you have a clearly stated gender preference, as in "We'd love to adopt a baby sister for little Phillip." If you haven't ruled out adopting a child of either sex, stay neutral and use the combined pronoun.

Be alert for any phrases that treat the child like a commodity, like "When we finally get a child," or "the baby we were meant to have." Choose instead statements sensitive to the life of the child, like "when we finally become parents," or "the baby who was meant to join our family." Similarly, avoid referring to the child as a "gift." Though they may look cute in ribbons and bows, a baby is never a package to be exchanged. The only gift that a birthmother is giving is to her child, and that's the best possible life she can provide.

Also, until the baby is placed for adoption, it belongs to the birthmother, both factually and psychologically. An involved birthmother is trying to find the right family for *her* child, not *a* child. Don't be afraid to cede ownership to her. There is no competition going on here; you and the birthmother are on the same team, trying to find the right home for her baby. Use the phrase *your baby*, even if it's psychologically difficult for you to do so.

Use Familiar Speech

Let birthmothers hear your real voice when you write. Most people's everyday writing is for business: the terse language of emails, the stilted formality of reports, or the scholarly voice they learned in school. Despite all your education and desire to employ Standard Written English, write your Dear Birthmother letter in as conversational a tone as possible.

Keep your vocabulary simple; you're not trying to impress your freshman English teacher. I'm not suggesting that you "talk down to" birthmothers; quite the opposite, I want you to respect their intelligence. But if you can say something simply and directly, then do so. A humorous old writing homily reminds, "Never use a long word when a diminutive one will do."

Don't be afraid of contractions. "We'd love it if you'd write to us" sounds more casual and immediate than "We would love it if you would write to us. " The latter sounds like a formal request. Choose language that is appropriate to both who you are and the subject at hand.

Take care not to assume too much informality, though. You're addressing someone you'd like to become your friend, but who isn't yet. A line like, "Hey girlfriend, how's the belly? Feelin' fat?" probably assumes too much.

Use Expressive Adjectives and Active Verbs

When writing a piece of limited length, you can't afford to waste words. It's important to make every word work for you as hard as it can. Verbs and adjectives provide the best opportunity to make your writing vivid and lively.

Never "like" when you can "love." Never "appreciate" when you can "cherish," "embrace," or "relish in." If you're not an enthusiastic person, so be it; I'm not trying to turn you into someone you are not. Just don't be lazy and settle for the easiest, most common verb. Dig a little. Work to find the right words to express the feelings you are trying to convey.

➤ **Dull**

I like walking.

> ## Lively

I enjoy walking

I love walking.

I adore walking.

I walk to stay healthy.

I derive great joy from my morning walk.

I delight in a brisk walk

Walking makes me feel wonderful.

Another habit that reveals a startling lack of imagination is to overuse forms of the verb, "to be." Professional editors call such a writer "The Wizard of Is." Sometimes you can't avoid using "to be" (and its conjugates: *am, are,* and *is*), but whenever possible, employ more active, interesting verbs. It will make your writing feel more alive.

The sample paragraph below suffers from excessive "is-ness." Two revisions follow. The first tries simply to eliminate as many instances of "to be" as possible; the second strives to substitute as many active verbs and expressive adjectives as possible. All three communicate essentially the same information. Compare them sentence by sentence to see how each improves upon the last.

> ## Original

John is a good writer, and I am happiest when I am sitting at home reading a book. We are a very quiet couple who are often found at home on Saturday night, in our living room that is very comfortable and pleasant. There are many benefits to the quiet life. The best is when we are listening to music together.

➢ **Revision #1**

John writes well, and I like to read. We're a quiet couple. On Saturday night, we enjoy quiet time together in our comfortable living room. Sometimes, we sit and listen to jazz; one of the many benefits the quiet life offers us.

➢ **Revision #2**

John writes well, and I love nothing better than a good book. As a quiet couple, our favorite Saturday night finds us curled up together in our cozy living room, snuggling to the music of Miles Davis and relishing the quiet life.

Each revision paints a more vivid image in your mind than the one before. Where the original describes a somewhat boring couple who sit around in silence every night, the last conjures a vibrant couple who are passionate about stillness and the life of the mind. Same couple, better writing. Notice also that both revisions employ about one-third fewer words than the original.

After you complete a draft of your letter, examine it paragraph by paragraph. Try to make each one as vivid as possible.

Employ Humor Gently

A little bit of gentle humor goes a long way toward making your letter warm and inviting. If it's a natural part of your character, let your personality and wit shine through when you write.

Humor can be a double-edged sword though. What's funny for some may be stupid–or worse–incomprehensible to others. Don't press it. Go for a smile, not for a guffaw.

LETTER FORMS

In this chapter, we'll examine the range of forms that potential adoptive parents commonly employ for their letters, as well as some creative variations. Each form is like a shell that contains your personal self-expression. Pick one that seems like a natural fit, or mix, match, and adapt them as you like. As with any type of writing, the form is less important than what you do with it.

Some people write better when following an outline or a structure; others find form constricting. Follow the path that's best for you. Either select a style before you begin, or simply start writing and let the form develop organically as you write. These forms are here to stimulate your imagination and orient you toward your goal. Perhaps you'll be inspired to invent your own approach. If you do, please send it to me so I can include it in future editions!

If you've already read a number of Dear Birthmother letters and are generally familiar with their various forms, then this chapter will help concretize what you already know. If you are new to the game, you might want to take a few minutes and flip to the appendixes in the back of the book. There, you'll find the complete text of many wonderful letters to browse through as a general introduction. If you have web access, I highly recommend you browse through the letters on <u>Adoption.com</u>, an excellent online registry with hundreds of letters posted, some good, some bad. The more you read, the more you'll recognize truly authentic writing.

He Says/She Says

The "he says/she says" letter is a very popular form, probably because of its flexibility and ease of use. The baseline voice speaks in the first person plural, "we," and then subsequent sections allow each partner to speak about their own life and their mate in personal terms.

A subhead to identify the speaker should precede each section. Typical sections include (for example): *About Us, About Heide, Heide on Jacob (or "I want to tell you about Jacob"), About Jacob, Jacob on Heide*, etc..

Here's an excerpt from a letter in this form. The full text appears on page 148.

About Us

We recently celebrated our 4th anniversary, but we met while volunteering two years before that. We quickly became best friends and have created a deeply loving marriage built upon respect, honesty, and trust. After three years of infertility, we are so excited and ready to adopt! We have so much love to give and are eager to nurture your baby and provide him or her with all the wonderful opportunities the world has to offer.

About Heide:

I grew up in the suburbs of Atlanta and currently work for a businessman, distributing his donations to local charities (basically, I get to give away somebody else's money!). I can't wait to be a stay-at-home mom. In my free time, I love to cook Italian food, entertain our wonderful friends, and volunteer at the local women's clinic.

I want to tell you about Jacob:

I fell in love with Jacob the moment I met him. His honesty, thoughtfulness, quick-witted charm shines through him. When he smiles and laughs his whole face lights up, and mine does too. He is always there to help me, my family, or even someone he doesn't know. Most of all, I love seeing the joy on Jacob's face when he plays with our nieces, teaches them new songs, or feeds our best friend's new baby. I love him very much, and I can't wait to see him caring for our child.

Subject

Another popular approach organizes the letter around subject headings, like *Home*, *Work*, and *Family*. Often you'll see this style combined with other forms. It's a great way to manage the flow of ideas and give your reader a comprehensive overview of your life.

Our lawyer has a great system for organizing Dear Birthmother letters. He asks his clients to address the various subject areas in the order of importance to them, and then tells his birthmothers that they have done so. In this way, everyone's on the same page, so to speak.

But even if birthmothers haven't been so informed, it makes good sense to organize your letter in this way. A good lead–the first few paragraphs of a piece—draws you into the story. A birthmother is more likely to read your letter all the way through if she's attracted to your lead. If you leave all the crucial stuff until the end, you risk her moving on in disinterest.

Here's an excerpt from a letter in subject form.

Why we want to Adopt

We've always wanted to be a mom and dad! Making a child laugh, seeing their beautiful smiles, holding their little hands, and giving them raspberries on their bellies all bring a special love that is so incredible.

When we learned we could not have children, we decided that adopting would make our dreams of becoming a family a reality. We can hardly wait for the journey to begin. And we want all of it, from rocking in our arms, wiping runny noses, comforting tears, and sharing in joys, to answering the endless questions like "Why is the sky blue?"

Our Home

We live in a great community: quiet, plenty of wide-open spaces, with a large park a block away. It's family oriented and safe, away from the craziness of the city (Los Angeles is an hour away). We also have one of the best school systems in California.

We own a large home, our "dream house," with lots of room to play and grow. It is on top of a hill overlooking the trees and mountains. On clear days, you can even see the ocean 20 miles away. In the mornings, bunnies scamper on the lawn, and Ruby brings out a big bag of peanuts to feed the squirrels and blue jays.

Our backyard gatherings are full of family and friends, especially on the 4ᵗʰ of July, when Jim grills up his famous baby-back ribs. He's definitely a kid magnet, and when he's not manning the grill, he's usually giving dolphin rides, playing Marco-Polo, or splashing around with them in our pool.

Blended Voice/Reporter

This is a straightforward approach, and though I admit it's my least favorite, it's one of the most popular. From a writing standpoint, it's a bit of a mixed bag. These letters are grounded in the third person voice common to newspaper reporting. People refer to themselves by first name, "he," and "she," as Ruby and Jim did in the previous sample. But rather than being consistent and referring to themselves collectively as "they," people often substitute "we," probably in an attempt to temper the impersonal nature of third person narrative.

As I've said before, the third-person voice generally keeps readers at a distance from events (appropriate for newspapers but deadly for personal letters), and also begs the question, "who is speaking?" Switching voices randomly has a jarring affect, pushing the reader away just as he or she gets drawn in.

Though a bit of a literary mess, this form does provide a convenient narrative structure, and it's so common, no one seems to notice its shortcomings. It also has a slightly more formal tone, which may suit you. If you do choose it, be sure to include a lot of specific detail and rich anecdotes to keep it intimate.

Here's an excerpt from a letter in blended voice/reporter form. The full text appears on page 155.

Maggie loves to read. She loves visiting the library and browsing bookstores. We both have a strong appreciation of the arts–music, art, literature, and dance–and we'll introduce our child to the wonderful opportunities for self-expression they can bring. One of Patrick's favorite pastimes is golf. He shares this hobby with his mother and father, who are already checking into Fisher-Price's line of toy golf clubs for the baby. Patrick also loves watching sports and looks forward to teaching our child to root for the New York and Catholic teams.

Guest Narrator

A terrific variation on the reporter style, this form employs an outside narrative voice to tell a couple's story. It's essentially a creative way of answering the question, "Who is talking to me?"

The example below, from a family looking to adopt a second child, uses the fictional narrative voice of their 18-month-old son by adoption. Since they chose a child's voice, it also gave them the opportunity to have some fun with it. I think this form could work just as well as written from the P.O.V. of a family pet.

You have to be careful not to get too cute, and not to pick a narrator who could be real (like your next-door neighbor). The fun comes from the fact that the reader understands that the letter is being written by the potential adoptive parents, although it's ostensibly about them.

Here's an excerpt from a letter in this form. The full text appears on page 158.

Bonjour! I'm Jean-Paul (they also call me Pépé) and I'm a year and half old. I'm writing this letter (true, Maurice and Regine, my parents are helping just a little bit) to tell you about our world and to say how much we would like to adopt your baby. I swear, I will be the best big brother in the whole wide world!

Dad and Mom met over ten years ago at an artsy-fartsy party and haven't been alone since. After ten years of marriage, they still love each other lots and lots, and have tons of fun together.

There is nothing traditional or usual about them, let me tell you. Dad is a director in the movie business and Mom is a writer. She is writing a book just for me and my future brother or sister. They like books and movies, gardens and the ocean. Mom loves growing roses and Dad loves to surf (I will someday, too). They both love to sail and look at the stars on a clear, summer night.

Two-Voice Dialog

I invented the two-voice style for my wife and I because I was restless trying to fit our story into any of the prevailing forms. I was trying to capture on the page the back-and-forth, balanced nature of our relationship.

The style, a variation of He says/She says, works for a number of reasons. First, it was organic for us (it's more or less what we sound like when you meet us). Second, it reads easily because it's written in a breezy, conversational style. Third, it's different, which helps it stand out from the crowd. And last, dialog reveals character, so "hearing" each of us speak in our own words reveals something additional about who we are.

It's organized by subject.

Here's an excerpt. The full text appears on page 137.

What's with the Bold and *Italics?*

Elicia and I both have a lot to say to you, and we wanted to find a way for you to hear both our voices in this letter. *We thought it would be fun to use italics when I (Elicia) am speaking,* and regular type when it's me (Nelson). *A lot of times, we want to say the exact same thing,* **so when it appears in bold type, we're both speaking together.**

Our Home

We live in a great neighborhood, quiet and hilly, with a park and recreation center near the lake at the bottom of the hill. *It's residential and safe, away from the craziness of the city. We also have one of the best elementary schools in the district.*

We own our home, a sweet little three bedroom, Spanish-style house. Elicia planted and tends our beautiful garden. *When we moved in, the place needed work. Nelson almost single-handedly remodeled the kitchen and downstairs. He's really good with tools.* We're both originally from New York, but have become addicted to the sunshine and warm climate in Los Angeles.

Mealtimes are special to us. We can both cook up a storm, and we take turns making delicious things. *I love that he's as good a cook as I am.* We look forward to dinner together. *Sometimes we sit in the dining room, and talk about the day, share our thoughts, or make plans for the weekend. Sometimes we watch TV, especially, it seems, during basketball season.* So sue me, I love the Lakers.

On weekends, we go out and play, or shop, or sometimes just putter in the garden. You should smell Elicia's roses! *On Sunday,*

I sing in the choir at church. I was raised in the Jewish religion. A spiritual life has always been important to us, although we haven't always been involved in organized religious practice. **Both of us feel that a child needs a moral and ethical education as well as an academic one.** *We're planning on exposing our children to the rich cultural traditions of both of our faiths.*

"10 things" List

This is a very creative idea. Essentially a subject organized letter; it takes a form common to magazine service articles, like a "tips" list. It's very accessible and easy to skim. Each "factoid" reads like a headline, followed by a short paragraph of detail.

Here's an excerpt from a letter in this form. The full text appears on page 163.

10 Things You'll Want to Know About Phyllis and Sam

1. We're committed to an Open Adoption.

We hope to have a life long connection with you. This includes letters, pictures, visits, etc. We believe open adoption is empowering to everyone involved, and we hope you feel that way too.

2. Phyllis will be a stay-at-home mom.

I was a nurse, but I want nothing more than to devote myself to providing a child with a stable home, chock full of love, attention, fun and daily adventures. Sam works as an accountant, but he plans to be home every night at 5:00 to spend lots of time with the baby.

3. Your child will be our first child.

But we'd love to adopt a second so that they can have some sibling fun. Both of us come from large families, and every year we join our brothers and sisters, and all their children (13 in all!) at our parents' house to celebrate a big Christmas morning. The kids all dress as elves and hand out the presents.

THE MAJOR SUBJECT AREAS

Now that we've covered form and style, it's time to address content. In this chapter, we'll examine the major subject areas you may want to explore in your resume. Not all of these areas need be addressed individually; but to write a comprehensive letter, you should try to touch on as many as you can, however briefly.

You may discover an opportunity within one area to discuss another (did you notice how my wife and I slipped our discussion of religion into a section called "Home"), but keep the flow of ideas clear and easy to follow. In general, complete one subject area before moving on to the next.

As we've discussed, not all letters are arranged by subject. Whatever style of letter you choose to create, the subject matter remains similar. Each section that follows is intended to illuminate an issue, help you understand birthmothers' point of view of it, and assist you in avoiding serious missteps.

Contact Information

Adoption professionals hold differing opinions about what contact information to make available and under what circumstances. I suggest you discuss with yours the types of outreach you/they plan to do and get an opinion about what they think appropriate. To be comprehensive, I will address the subject with an eye toward maximal availability.

What contact information you choose to include is up to you, *how* you choose to include it remains constant. The golden rule in all matters of communication with birthmothers is: **Be easily reachable.** Unless the professional you're working with gives you another format to follow, put the following information just above your greeting on the cover sheet or on the first page of your letter:

➤ **Names (First or first and last)** (*see below*)

➤ **Contact phone number(s)**

➤ **Email address (optional, but recommended)**

➤ **Lawyer/Facilitator/Agency Name**

➤ **Lawyer/Facilitator/Agency contact phone number**

Then, at the bottom of each succeeding page, put your name and contact number again. This way, a birthmother can still contact you if she loses the first page of your letter.

Get a special, dedicated email address to use solely for adoption. If you're on AOL, add a new screen name to your account. If you can access the internet at work, consider setting up a free, web-based email account. Some will forward mail to your main account, thus saving you the trouble of regularly checking different mailboxes. A number of adoption web sites also offer addresses, an option I favor. Make sure it's an account you can check a couple of times a day (again, depending on what type of outreach you are doing).

Opening Paragraphs

The writer would be a rich man indeed who can offer a definitive answer to the question, How to begin? A great author once said, "the goal of the first sentence is to get to the second sentence."

Opening paragraphs are as individual as the person writing them. In general, your opening should be like a big hug–warm, open, and inviting. You can address almost any subject you like, but the strongest approach reaches out to your reader simply and graciously and welcomes them to your world. A little enthusiasm doesn't hurt either.

Avoid leading with sorrow: "We know how terrible you must feel," "This is a difficult time," "It hurts so much when we think about a baby." Imagine a birthmother reading fifteen letters that all begin by telling her how badly she feels and you'll understand the most compelling reason for embracing a sunny and positive outlook.

> **Here are some examples** *(in italics)*, **with my comments to the right of each :**

We are excited about fulfilling our lifelong dream of parenthood and are thrilled and grateful that you would consider allowing us to welcome your baby into our lives. We can provide your child with a loving home environment, lots of hugs and fun times, and a good spiritual and moral foundation to help him/her grow up to be a happy, self-confident adult.

A very strong, confident statement of self.

We hope that this letter and these pictures will give you some idea of the loving and secure home we can provide for your baby. We have been married for 14 years, and our love for each other continues to grow stronger every day. We have always dreamt of having children, but we're not able to conceive on our own. Now we happily look forward to adoption so we can share our love with a new life.

A gentle way of mentioning infertility without dwelling on it.

They call it "THE week with Jane and Stu." We call it a lot of fun. For three summers, our teenage cousin and nephew have spent a week with us while attending baseball camp. During these visits, we learned to make sure they got to bed on time, to say 'no' to the extra boxes of Ho-Ho's at the grocery store, to cheer them up when they had a bad day at the plate, and to celebrate their camp awards. Through these wonderful times, we have gained a taste of the pleasures (as well as the challenges) of parenting. We now realize how much we will enjoy loving and raising our own children.

I love this opening. It brings you into their story effortlessly and makes you want to keep reading.

Welcome to our hearts and home, where love is unconditional, promises are kept, dreams are chased, passions are followed, fun is to be had, and the world is made a better place step by step!

Great, clear writing. Lots of enthusiasm. You get the immediate feeling that these people know who they are.

We admire the courage it took to give your child the gift of life and your selflessness in making an adoption plan. Your baby is so blessed to have a mother who loves him or her so much. We know that you want your child to grow up well cared for, in a loving family, with every opportunity to succeed. We hope that you will come to believe what we already know in our hearts-we can provide your child the loving, secure, happy home of which you dream.

A good hug. Strong and embracing. If you're going to assume anything about your birthmother, assume she cares.

Thank you for reading our letter! We're Juan and Victoria and we are excited about becoming a family. We know you love your baby very much and we are grateful for your courage and your commitment to considering an adoption plan. We hope that, with your help, we can give your baby a wonderful home.

Leads with a great sense of communality and cooperation. Very respectful of birthmothers, and very positive about the process.

A Few Tips:

➢ **Name**

Providers disagree about whether or not you should provide your last name to potential birthmothers before you meet them. Some argue that omitting it seems like you have something to hide, while others feel that first-names-only provides you with a bit more protection and privacy at the start. In a so-called "semi-open" adoption, you never reveal your last name.

Follow the guidance of your adoption professional on this issue. My suggestion would be to omit your last names on any communication available for general dissemination, and consider including them in any private distribution by you or your adoption professional.

➢ **Contact numbers**

If you are comfortable with the idea of speaking with birthmothers, **list a number at which a birthmother can contact you directly.** Some will be averse to contacting a lawyer, agency, or other part of "the system" until they have grown comfortable with you directly. Include your professional's number for those who feel just the opposite. Either way, it takes a lot of courage for them to pick up the phone and make that call. Make sure they can reach a real person (not a machine) at all times.

Make it possible for them to contact you with little inconvenience and at no expense to them. The mess that passes for our telephone system these days gives you myriad options, though getting them to work together sometimes takes a bit of doing. It's worth the effort.

First, get a toll-free, "800" number that rings at your home. All long distance providers offer some type of service. Some are very inexpensive to set up or even free. You may even be able to set it up so that your phone sounds a distinct ring when someone calls your toll-free number.

Then, use a call forwarding service to forward the number to where you can be reached, work or cell phone (provided you are somewhere that you can take a call), at all times. Most local phone companies offer some type of easy call forwarding service.

Your goal is to arrange it so that you are as "connected" as you can be, as often as you can be, and for it to be as easy as possible for a birthmother to reach you at any time of day or night. Depending on what type of outreach you are doing, a birthmother might be in a different time zone, work second shift, not work at all, only be able to access a private phone after her Mom goes to sleep, not have a callback number, etc. You will dramatically reduce your chances of being out of touch by providing a single number for birthmothers to call and using the technology at your disposal to assure that the call reaches you, wherever you are.

> **Email address**

Better than half the country now has full-time access to the internet, and just about anyone can walk into a local library and log on, so providing some means of digital contact makes good sense. My wife and I found that there were a number of birthmothers who felt uncomfortable picking up the phone and calling us, but were put at ease after we exchanged a couple of emails to get to know each other. We ended up finding the birthmother of our son that way.

We are very excited about expanding our family again through the adoption process. We are a very happy, loving family, enjoy being together, and all eagerly await the day another spirit joins our family. We admire your decision to choose adoption, and we hope that we can help fulfill your desire to find a loving family for your child.

I like how simple this is, and especially the last sentence. It says, "we're here to be the solution."

Why Adoption?

This is one of the most important subjects you must address in your letter, and you should do it early on. Immediately following your opening is a good spot.

This is your opportunity to express the joy and excitement you feel at the prospect of building your family through adoption. Discuss your involvement with other children, your dreams of family, and why this is the right choice for you. Above all, **be positive**. Although she may be making an adoption plan, a birthmother may still harbor doubts or ambiguities, and may be turned off to you if your doubts reinforce hers. Communicate through your positive embrace of adoption that you have no negative stigma attached to it, and that her child will be loved and cherished when they join your family.

You can touch on your infertility story here, but don't get bogged down in sorrow (*see A Word on Need, page 97*), and don't go into excessive detail (number of IVFs, loss of baby, etc.). It's enough to offer infertility as a reason why you've embraced adoption.

If you have completed a state-approved home study, you could mention it within this context. Though most birthmothers will not be sufficiently immersed in the adoption process to understand what this means, there is a small minority for whom it will be a positive factor. If it doesn't seem natural to mention it here, it's not a bad idea to slip it in somewhere. Don't make a big deal about it, bragging that you are "state-approved" as if it were the Good Housekeeping Seal of Approval. Just mention that you've completed this step and move on.

The main thing to avoid here is to speak about adoption as a consolation prize or a fall back plan. If the first draft of your letter sounds something like, "Well, we couldn't conceive, so adoption was all that was left to us," then you've got some personal work to do. Like birthmothers, it is normal for you at this stage to be wrestling still with issues surrounding adoption, either because you come from an experience with infertility, or because you simply don't know much about it. This is one of those Dorian Gray moments; what you write quickly reflects what's going on in your heart.

> **Here's an example of a typical "consolation prize" paragraph:**

Shortly after we were married, we knew we wanted to start a family. Unfortunately, after four years of infertility treatments that included in-vitro fertilization, we have not had the success of becoming pregnant. We have had many failures and disappointments while undergoing infertility treatments, although our relationship has grown stronger and closer than ever. Throughout our infertility treatments, we have realized that if we were never blessed with a child in our lives, we would never experience one of the greatest joys in life, that of parenting a child. This is something that we do not want to miss. Because, more than anything else, we want to provide love, stability, and happiness to a child, we decided that adoption would fulfill us in reaching our goal of becoming parents.

> **Here's the same information written with a positive embrace-ment of adoption:**

We knew we wanted to start a family shortly after we were married, and believe parenting a child will be one of the great joys of life. Our four years of infertility have strengthened our relationship and we are closer than ever as we begin our adoption journey. We can't wait to become parents, and we feel adoption will give us the opportunity to share our love, stability, and happiness with a child.

If you are looking in the mirror at this stage and seeing conflicts in either you or your partner's face, or if your first draft sounds more like the former example than the latter, I would highly recommend you begin to actively process these feelings, either alone or with the help of an adoption counselor. Conflicted feelings will affect the way you interact with birthmothers, from your letter onwards.

Does that mean that you should put down this book and go no further with your adoption efforts until you're absolutely clear about how you feel? Speaking from a purely human standpoint (removing financial considerations for the moment), I would say no. If you think that adoption is a real possibility for you, then proceed as best you can in spite of any ambiguity you feel. Adoptions take time and feelings change. When an opportunity does arise, you can always say no if you're not ready.

Pre-adoption counseling can help you work through your (understandable) conflicts, pain, or sense of loss. Knowledge is power.

It will help you come to a place where you either truly feel that adoption is the right way for you to build a family, or not. You'll then be able to act with an open heart.

Openness

It's a good idea to address the issue of openness somewhere in your letter, even if only to "tip your hat" to the issue.

According to adoption professionals, the most successful open adoptions occur when potential adoptive parents and birthparents form a close prebirth relationship. Your Dear Birthmother letter should always reflect a willingness on your part to make this most immediate of prebirth times as easy as possible for your birthmother.

Post-birth relationships are more individual, and more complex. It's not appropriate in this book to present a long discussion about various types of post-birth, open adoption relationships. I recommend that you examine this issue with your adoption professional to gain a clearer understanding of the possibilities. I will say that it is normal at this stage in your adoption journey to have fear, uncertainty, or doubt about a post-adoption relationship with birthparents. After all, you haven't yet met these people. How can you say whether, and to what degree, you want them to participate in your family's life?

This same anxiety grips birthparents; they don't know you either. Birthparents who choose open adoption often do so because they want to have say in who raises their child. The challenge of finding the right family is a source of anxiety for them, and this can translate into heightened up-front interest in the openness of the adoption. It's often the first question they'll ask when you speak. It isn't, however, usually the deciding factor in their choice. In most cases, as you get to know each other, your personal relationship with your birthmother takes a front seat and anxieties ease. The trust and communication you build will enable you to discuss this issue when the proper time comes.

In your Dear Birthmother letter, **demonstrate a gentle deference to the birthmother's wishes in this area.** For the purposes of an introductory letter, you want the birthmother to feel that she will not have a problem discussing this issue with you and that you will be open to her feelings.

Resist being too specific about your openness plans at this stage, even if you have strong feelings about them. Your views may change as you get to know your birthmother better and not all birthmothers will want a continued open relationship. Some fear the idea of a post-birth relationship and retreat from anyone trying to force it on them; they would prefer to get on with their lives and don't want to be reminded of the past. Being general (and deferential) in this area keeps the door open to further discussion.

Adoption professionals I spoke with were unanimous, however, in the feeling that you should **never suggest the possibilities of post-adoption visits within the context of a Dear Birthmother letter.** For a number of reasons too complex to discuss in this forum, it was strongly suggested that to do so often leads to catastrophic consequences for the success of the placement. If you are strongly committed to the idea of post-adoption visits, discuss thoroughly with your adoption professional the proper time and place to have such discussions.

> ➤ **Here are a few good examples of the openness issue:**

You may wonder what the baby's future might be like with us, and we'd like to tell you about the love and opportunities that we could share with this special child. We like the idea of openness to honor you, and will work with you in this area to respect your wishes.

Simple, gracious, deferential.

Through the process of adopting Georgia, we learned that birthparents and adoptive families have all kinds of relationships with one another and that what is most important is for everyone to feel comfortable and to do what is right for their situation. We grew close with Georgia's birthmother; she truly broadened our outlook on life, love and family. We're open to letting our relationship with you take its own natural course, as well.

This couple used the specific story of their first birthmother relationship as a way of discussing how wonderful open adoption can be. But they were wise enough to maintain a healthy respect and open mind regarding another birthmother's wishes.

We believe that families created by adoption are special and should be honored. Our children will always know their adoption stories and the wonderful way we became a family.

A very respectful attitude.

We have an open attitude towards adoption and are willing to be as much of a part of your pregnancy as you are comfortable with us being. We also agree to send a letter and photos at six months, then once a year following to keep you apprised on the growth of your baby.

I like the willingness to participate in the pregnancy, and the deference to the birthmother's wishes in this area. However, I think it's unnecessary to be this specific about further contact. It makes you seem unnecessarily rigid and inflexible.

Child Rearing

Maybe there are child-free couples out there who sit around dreaming of children and discussing in detail how they will educate, discipline, culture, and introduce them to the world, but I don't know any of them. If you are such a person, you have a leg up here; writing this section will be a simple exercise in transcribing what you already know.

For the rest of us, there are certain things about adoption that seem plainly unfair, and talking about how you are going to raise your child before s/he arrives is one of them. There is no law asking biological parents to produce such a plan before being permitted to leave the hospital, so why should adoptive parents be required to?

Unfortunately (or fortunately, depending on how you look at it), we are. Your Dear Birthmother letter is the first place you will be called upon to do so, and in most cases, your state-required home study or parent preparation will be the second. The unexpected fact is that this process can be fun.

Sit down with your mate and dream. I suggest a good meal, a nice bottle of wine, and a quiet night with your spouse. If you're coming out the other side of infertility, there's a good chance you haven't done much of this, so think of this exercise as a positive step in your healing process. There's a baby coming, and it's time to embrace that fact, maybe even giggle a little about it. Jot down notes. Even if you don't end up using too many of these details in your letter, you will almost certainly be asked something specific by a birthmother, like "will you spank your children," so it's beneficial to have thought about it in advance.

In your letter, keep the discussion general and philosophical. Include specific details only in a positive light, especially if they reveal something about who you are, i.e., "and of course, John will be working on the baby's curve ball as soon as s/he can get a grip."

> ➤ **Here are a few good examples:**

We'll raise our children in much the same way we were raised: a positive outlook toward life, lots of encouragement, lots of love, abundant warm hugs, and adoring kisses. We will guide and nurture them to grow, thrive, and become their unique and special selves. We will trust them, and give them space to be responsible and make the right decisions. We'll show them that even when things don't go as planned; the result is just as good and usually better.

This last line is especially good, applicable as it is to the birthmother's situation as well.

We believe that children should be raised through love and understanding, guidance and teaching, plenty of patience and a good dose of humor. We believe in teaching children, from the earliest age, the wonders of learning, the value of family, and the importance of kindness and respect. We believe that kids should learn to play hard, to study and work hard and, above all, to have a light heart, an open mind, and a ready smile.

A statement of belief like this reveals your core values in a wonderful manner.

What does all this mean on a daily level? We want our children to have fun positive experiences. As babies, they'll have toys and games that challenge them physically and mentally in a warm, safe environment. We'll encourage them to be creative and work with others. We'll expose them to all types of music, books, and sports. We'll teach them to play ball and swim. We'll do chores together too. We'll take out the trash and mow the lawn. We'll wash the dogs. We'll sing. We'll celebrate holidays. As they grow, we'll

I love how active this paragraph is. Combined, as it was in the letter, with a more general statement of beliefs, it just sweeps you up in its energy and positive outlook. Though it is a list, the sheer specificity of it tells you a lot about this couple.

(more)

(cont.)

go to church together and volunteer together. We'll teach them to cook healthy food and we'll eat together. We'll support them when they struggle, applaud them when they do well and guide them when they make mistakes. We will love them every day.

Education

Most birthmothers want their children to have as many advantages in life as possible, either because they themselves were raised that way, or because their inability to provide them factors into their reasons for placing. Education is a lifetime ticket to opportunity.

Learning is a family activity. Do you remember how wonderful it felt when your Dad helped you with your homework? Discuss the role education played in your life, and its importance to your view of raising a child.

Don't get too bogged down listing your own scholastic achievements—universities attended, degrees earned, and the like—this isn't a job application. Education means different things to different people. It's not always about school; it's about the life of the mind. Speak about the values you want to convey to your children, the experiences you hope to share, and the places you want to visit. Speak about growing, and discovering, and learning what it is to be human.

Work

Before you have a family, it's common to define yourself by what you do. Think about the times you meet new people, and how often the first thing you talk about is your job. At the risk of gender stereotyping, men are particularly susceptible to this habit.

As this is not Victorian England, there is little chance that your child will accompany you to work anytime soon, so make sure you don't devote so much attention to writing about work that it seems your child will not have a family life. Work may be the most important thing in your life, but within the context of a Dear Birthmother letter, it should appear in balance with your other pastimes. Birthmothers are trying to picture their child's life, not the father- or mother-shaped hole you will seem to be if you insist on bragging about your overtime hours.

Avoid getting sucked into a recitation of your professional *curriculum vitae*. Don't mention how much money you make; it seems like bragging, and besides, numbers are meaningless out of context. $100,000 per year in Los Angeles or New York means one thing, and in Little Rock, something altogether different. This is one of the few places where a general statement about your job and relative financial comfort level is best.

A lot of us have jobs or job titles where what we do is either not self-evident or has bad associations attached to it. In these cases, try to describe your job in the simplest possible terms, and use the opportunity to make a more vivid point about your lifestyle.

Here's a good example. Patrick works in a call center, training and supervising teams of telephone salespeople. He's extremely likeable, but someone casually reading about his job might make the wrong assumption about him, and unless you know something about sales, the idea of a "call center" is murky at best. Here's how he turned a possible problem into a positive.

> *Patrick works in marketing, where he teaches a group of 25 agents the art of sales. He has been very successful, mostly because people trust him right away. He's close with his co-workers, many of whom have small children. Company picnics are really fun since there are lots of little kids running around and playing. Our children will get to play with kids from a variety of cultures and backgrounds.*

This paragraph paints a picture of a close family of workers from a variety of backgrounds, with Patrick as a sort of father figure among them. It makes two good points about sales, that he's successful at it and that people trust him, ameliorating two possible negative assumptions. Best of all, it paints vivid pictures of both a working father who will be actively involved in his children's life and of happy children at play.

Working parents vs. Stay-at-homes

If you're planning on being a stay-at-home mother or father for all or part of your child's life, say so. Many adoption professionals report that this is an important factor to some birthmothers.

If doing so, however, means making great sacrifices in your lifestyle, it will only confuse issues if you try to describe them in too much detail. Avoid a sentence like:

> *Sylvia is going to quit her job as an investment banker to be a stay-at-home mom, so we'll be selling our beautiful house and moving into a small apartment where we will survive on my salary as poet laureate of Evanston, IL. That's how important it is to us.*

Consider something a bit simpler, like:

Being a stay-at-home mom is really important for Sylvia, and we're going to do whatever it takes to give our baby that kind of constant attention and care through his early years.

If you are not going to be a stay-at-home Mom household, stop fretting (I know you are). The fact is that in almost two-thirds of two-parent American families, both parents work. Most are proud of this...until you mention raising a child. Then a strange set of Daddy Knows Best stereotypes erupts like a boil and previously high-functioning people suddenly question all the choices they've made in their lives. Know that only twenty-nine percent of American households still conform to this stereotype, a number that's decreased twelve percent in the last ten years.

There are lots of ways to raise a child well, as many different models as there are couples to raise them. All families change over time in response to both opportunity and demand. If you're tempted to skirt the fact that the woman of the family is not a traditional housefrau, get over it.

Present the positive aspects that a working woman brings to a family in terms of self-esteem, self-reliance, and the fully enfranchised role of women in society. Some birthmothers come from a world where "traditional" upbringing is still the norm, or at least, the cliche of the norm, and plenty of others can't imagine a mom that *doesn't* work. By addressing your work life head on in positive terms, you normalize it, and open the door for further discussion.

No matter what your professional life, a heartfelt and thoughtful statement about how you plan to manage your family/work balance demonstrates competence and a mature approach to child rearing.

> ➤ **Here are some good examples of statements by both one- and two-income families.**

When we become parents, the needs of our family will direct Samantha's decisions regarding work. She has already reduced her work commitments due to our marriage and planning for a family. As a pediatric therapist, she can arrange a flexible schedule. My employer allows me several weeks of family leave, and I can reduce my work schedule to part time to enjoy the transition into parenthood.

This hits the nail on the head. A professional couple willing to make the changes necessary to become a family.

I enjoyed my years in the Navy, but family is more important, so I am happy to be settled here in Seattle. For the past several years, I have worked as an industrial mechanic for a large company here in town, and I attend the University at night to earn my degree in Anthropology. I work a four-day workweek, which gives me an extra day off, so I will put it to good use taking care of the baby in my new role as "Dad."

Good example of using "work facts" to share something more personal with the reader.

I am a Doctor of natural medicine, a Chiropractor and Nutritionist. Upon the arrival of our child, I plan to retire and become a full-time and (very happy) mom. Steve is very supportive and will make a wonderful father. He works as a building contractor and property manager and comes from a family of successful businesspersons. His schedule is very flexible and being a Dad will be his first priority.

A great statement by someone who will make the transition to being a stay-at-home Mom.

Like most families today, we both work. It allows us to live a comfortable lifestyle, own our own home and to provide for the future of our family. We both have a very strong work ethic and enjoy our professions. Although we work hard throughout the day, we feel that evenings and weekends should be dedicated to family time and family activities. It's important for us to provide the best possible opportunities for our children.

A positive avocation of values, this couple is not afraid to say who they are and what they believe. Yet they clearly recognize the importance of home life.

Frank has worked as an administrator at the University for 20 years. His office is only 10-minutes from home and he spends lunch every day with Kate. Cecilia works part time for a wonderful organization that researches children's issues. She stayed home for 18 months after Kate was born and will take time off to be with the new baby, too. When she returns to work, she has the option of reducing her hours or working from home occasionally.

On the days she works, Gertie, a wonderful woman with more than 20 years of child care experience, takes care of Kate in our home. Kate adores Gertie. She crawls in her lap for a big hug as soon as she arrives, then they go out to the playground, to "tot lot" or to the bookstore for story hour. Gertie is just like another member of the family.

Tackles the child care issue head on, and while this may be more detail than is required for an introduction, it reveals a forthrightness and honesty that tells you something essential about this couple.

Volunteer Work

In a document that is essentially self-centered, mentioning your volunteer work gives you a welcome opportunity to talk about helping others and to show that you care about things outside yourselves. Include as much detail as you feel appropriate to the activity's place in your life. If you volunteer with kids, discuss your interaction with them and what you have learned that will make you better parents.

Marriage/Relationship

At a minimum, your resume should mention how long you've been married and what is special about your current marriage. Many couples live together before getting married, so don't be afraid to add in those years, too ("married for three years, but together for eight"). Most birthmothers, in their attempt to secure a stable home for their child, place a high premium on the length and strength of potential adoptive parents' relationship. Be specific.

Talk about your relationship in terms that are natural to you, and don't be too afraid of relationship cliches like, "We're best friends as well as lovers," or, "We knew from the first that we were soul mates." Back up the statement with a specific example of what you mean. Find the level of sentimentality that feels appropriate to you. If greeting card poems are your idea of romance, go for it. A birthmother who shares your feelings will probably contact you. The only sin here is to tip the scales too far toward the romantic out of some preconception that birthmothers are all starry-eyed, romantic little girls. Remember, they're just like you.

Some professionals advocate always including "how we met"

stories. These can be great opportunities to talk about each other's flattering attributes in a natural context. Wedding stories also do this well. The more specific and detailed the story, the more likely that the reader will begin to see you as you saw each other in those special moments.

Don't equivocate when talking about your marriage. Every relationship has its difficulties, and the future holds no guarantees for anyone. But your Dear Birthmother letter is not the place for an in-depth analysis of all that could be better in your partnership. There is such a thing as too much honesty, especially when you are first introducing yourself to someone. Remember the party bore?

Keep in mind that many (though not all) birthmothers do not have an active partner in their lives, and will be attracted to what makes the bond between you and your mate unique. You'll transmit this information subliminally throughout the letter in the way that you describe your lives together.

Home

Home is a concept, not a building. Speaking about home speaks to stability, domesticity, nurturing, and family. Most birthmothers are looking for reassurance in this area, and for an idea of what her child's home life will be like.

Begin by briefly describing where you live. Avoid sounding like a realty listing.

➤ **Good**

We have a three-bedroom home on the top of a hill with a great backyard for the kids to play in.

Our apartment building is full of families with small kids, so our son or daughter will have lots of friends to play with, and lots of watchful eyes keeping him safe.

We live in a two-bedroom walk-up in a great old neighborhood in the city, close to a big park and just a ten-minute subway ride from the children's museum.

Our cute little Cape Cod bungalow is on a quiet street in a great, culturally mixed neighborhood.

> **Realtor-itis:**

We have a three-bedroom, two-bath, California Ranch-style house with a family room, two-car garage, step-down living room, and fireplace on a half-acre wooded lot on the south side of town. The house features coved ceilings and many built-ins, as well as wall-to-wall carpeting in the bedrooms.

If you rent an apartment, don't spend a second playing "keeping up with the Joneses." Lots of wonderful people live in apartments. Trumpet your life proudly and focus on what's important: love, caring, nurturing, and stability.

Home is more than a house. It encompasses your entire domestic life, your neighborhood, and your friends. What are the schools like? Are their parks nearby? Cultural Attractions? What do you do around the house on weekends? Do you garden, tinker with cars, remodel the house, or do the Sunday crossword puzzle? Describe how your child will fit into these activities. Talk about mealtimes, always a source of people's warmest family memories. Paint a picture of how you dream them to be when your children join your family.

> ## Here are some good examples:

We live in a nice, family-oriented neighborhood that is close to the ocean and near a large park. The park has a swimming pool, a pond with ducks to feed, a playground, and sport fields. The school district ranks among the top in the state. Our bright and cheery home has a big backyard ready to be filled with toys, although the kids will have to share it with our other family members: Viva, a sweet Labrador Retriever dog and Llrona, a big black cat. Viva loves kid, gives lots of slurpy kisses, and makes for a warm and fuzzy pillow. Llrona, which means "cry-baby" in Spanish, likes to make her presence known with her loud meow.

We live near a large university in Boston in a neighborhood filled with interesting people who come from all over the world to learn and work. We love living in the city and take advantage of all of its wonders, including museums, festivals, sports, and cultural attractions of every kind. We own a large, three-bedroom, condominium in a charming one hundred-year-old six flat with a huge backyard. The families in our building are very friendly, and most of our neighbors have small children. We have a playground at either end of the block. There are over a half dozen excellent preschools in the neighbor hood and classes in music, art, and dance are readily available. There are also soccer and softball teams for kids of all ages, and we are only a mile from the riverfront bike paths and greenbelt.

We live in a spacious one level house in suburban Middle Tennessee, with plenty of room to play both indoors and in the big back yard. Jackson has the workshop of his dreams in the basement where he spends hours hammering, sawing, and painting to his heart's content. Cynthia's favorite room is the library, where we have shelves filled floor to ceiling with books: ask her a question, she can find the answer! There's a big, bright nursery decorated with Peanuts characters just waiting for a new arrival. Beautiful big old trees fill the neighborhood, and in the springtime, we love sitting on our deck surrounded by the fresh green leaves. In the fall, our child will have all the leaf piles they could want to jump and play in.

Extended Family

There is an old proverb–either African or Native American depending on who you believe–that says, "It takes a whole village to raise a child." At no time will this be more apparent to you than the day you arrive home with your baby. Mark my words: even if you hate your family today, tomorrow they will be angels from heaven if they show up to meet the baby bearing casseroles.

Although this isn't a parenting book and I'm no expert, here's a sound bit of advice from one new parent to another. Repeat after me: "Sure, we'd love to have you over to meet little Pipsqueak..., bring food." Having a baby is a great way to lose weight. Why? The first few weeks are such delicious, exhaustive chaos that you often just forget to eat. Your best friend in the world becomes the one who brings the biggest pan of microwave-ready baked ziti with meatballs.

Extended family interests birthmothers. They may be looking for the benefits that extended family brings, or they may have some trepidation as to how they will accept your adopted child.

If your parents are alive, make sure you talk about "Grandma and Grandpa." The image of a multigenerational family provides a sense of stability and continuity. Besides, someone has to spoil the kid. If there are other rug-rats crawling around the family, mention them too. There's nothing better than a cousin to play with occasionally.

If your extended family is geographically remote or not involved with your life, take a moment to describe the "chosen" family, your friends and associates that will surround the child's life. Our son has lots of "aunts" and "uncles" who are as attached to him as any blood relative. Many of them are now more interested in coming to see him than to see us.

Do be careful not to oversell in this area. Commonly, people make the mistake of going into an endless litany of names and relations. This isn't the twelfth book of the Iliad. Just describe the general involvement of family and their importance in your life and the life of the baby.

Include your pets. In most people's mind, domestic animals, especially ones you can cuddle, are metaphors for children. In fact, I'm sure you know people who treat their animals better than they treat their kids. If you keep snakes, ferrets, frogs, or any other animal that someone might construe as either potentially dangerous to a child or just plain icky, you should probably omit mention of them. It's simpler than trying to explain how safe or affectionate you believe them to be. You can talk all you want, but you'll never convince me to hug a frog.

Being a cat person myself, I would put pit bulls, mastiffs, Dobermans, and any other really scary dogs in this same category. Why risk activating someone's fears unnecessarily? Then again, I know that dog owners are a different breed. There may be a birthmother out there who was raised with a pit bull and can't imagine life without one. She may be the right birthmother for you. My general advice about scary or non-cuddly pets is better safe than sorry. Ultimately, though, it's up to you.

> ## Here are some examples:

David's seven brothers and sisters have a total of 16 kids, so we're the most experienced aunt and uncle you could imagine! We love to spend holidays at his dad's home on Cape Cod with the extended family so we can play with all our nieces & nephews. His two sisters expect babies this year, so the child we adopt will have two little cousins close in age.

Good opportunity to mention your involvement with kids.

Though our extended families live far away, we have a large circle of close friends that we consider "chosen" family, and they can't wait for us to be parents. Our child will have rafters of "aunts" and "uncles," especially at holiday time. We've been gathering for a huge Thanksgiving potluck feast for years now. Everyone brings a dish that they are "famous" for. Stan makes the turkey (brining it so that it's really moist) and I make the best cranberry sauce in the country (at least that's what Stan tells me).

Everything is positive. Even family far away can be turned into an asset. Good anecdote.

Our family is a huge part of our lives, and we spend lots of time with them. Ruby's family all lives within 30 minutes and Jim's is only 4 hours away. Our parents can't wait for another grandchild. They all love being surrounded by the family. Like when Jim's parents stayed at our house for a week to celebrate their 50th anniversary. The yummy smells of Mom's famous roast lamb and fresh baked pie (from apples we picked off our own tree) filled the house. A wonderful, loving week, it included a trip to the zoo with our nieces & nephews and lots of laughs.

Good anecdote. Good specificity.

Religion

Perhaps because of the state of organized religion in the U.S., the "R" question causes consternation for many potential adoptive parents. For those with a strong spiritual practice, describing the role religion plays in your life may be quite simple. Those of you whose spirituality or religious affiliation is less defined may find the structure of a Dear Birthmother letter an awkward place to discuss these complex issues.

For non-Christians, being up-front about your religious background can pose a particular dilemma. Birthmothers come from all over the country and a variety of backgrounds, and some have no personal experience of Jewish, Moslem, Buddhist, or other minority religions. The brief nature of a Dear Birthmother letter makes it an inadequate forum to introduce someone to the complexity of these beliefs. Yet, to simply state your religious affiliation without attendant explanation could open you to stereotype or misunderstanding.

Misconception in the area of religion runs both ways, For example, my wife and I are essentially secular humanists raised in different religious backgrounds—she, Congregationalist, and I, Jewish. Early on in our adoption journey, we were contacted by a birthmother who began the conversation by saying, "I was raised Catholic, what religion are you?"

Petrified that we were going to alienate this woman right off the bat, we swallowed hard and patiently explained our personal spirituality and that we planned to expose our children to both of our cultural traditions (neither of which bears any resemblance to Catholicism). Then we held our breath.

She paused a second. "Good," she said, "I'm looking for anyone who's not Catholic."

We had to laugh, not at her wishes, but at how wrong our supposition had been. It taught us a valuable lesson about preconceptions, and we never had a problem discussing religion with a birthmother again.

We were up-front about our beliefs in our Dear Birthmother letter, and because we expressed them in a positive light, a different birthmother, from rural South Carolina, later felt comfortable enough to ask me directly, "What do Jews do?" Having never met any, she just simply didn't know. It led to a wonderful discussion that built trust between us.

When it comes to religion, remember that birthmothers are just like you. Some have very strong feelings about how they want their children raised and some are indifferent. But almost all birthmothers want to learn your views, and you should seriously consider discussing how your spirituality will fit into the life of your child. To my eye, letters that omit reference to religion seem to be avoiding something. Be as direct or as oblique as you feel appropriate, but be as clear as you can. Remember that the goal is to find the right birthmother for you. She will be the one whose views in this area mesh well with yours.

Adoption professionals strongly recommend that those who choose to treat religion in a nonspecific way in their letter make sure to clarify the subject early on in their birthmother relationship. A sudden discovery by a birthmother that the adoptive parents she believed were ordinary Protestants turned out to be Catholic, or Buddhist, or Jewish, or Agnostic can lead to unfortunate consequences. If you mention God, assume that a birthmother will think it's a Christian God.

(This is a good note to heed in relation to any potential "negative aspect," such as multiple divorces, older children, past substance abuse issues, etc. If you are vague about them in your letter, make sure you get your adoption providers advice about the appropriate context in which to clarify them with your birthmother before the birth of the baby. The best adoptions are built on no surprises.)

➢　**Here are some different ways people have handled the R-word:**

Our spirituality plays an important role in our lives. Although Patrick is Catholic and Maggie is a Religious Scientist, we both respect each other's beliefs and often

Gives you insight into both their cooperative nature and their individuality.

(more)

(cont.)

attend services together, which we will continue to do as a family. Our beliefs have so much in common, and the differences make for some spirited discussions.

We hope you find peace in the knowledge that the life growing inside you will be loved and cherished. May God bless you and give you comfort and strength. You may not feel like a hero, but you are a hero to us. Without brave people like you, Michael and I would not even have a chance to love a child of our own. We are ever so grateful for the chance you are giving us.

This closing paragraph demonstrates spirituality without getting specific about anything. It lays on the sentiment pretty thickly, but if that's an accurate reflection of who they are, then it's okay. This couple must be careful to explain their beliefs to any birthmother with whom they connect.

Though we don't belong to any organized religion, we both are very spiritual people. We find our inner peace in the sun shining through the trees, or a hummingbird on the wing. We plan to raise our children with a great appreciation of all that is good in the world and with all its mysteries as well.

A great secular humanist's statement.

We met at a Lutheran college and are now "regulars" at our Lutheran church. We sit in the same pew almost every Sunday; it gives Jack a great angle to make faces at our niece and nephew during the service. We help with worship by reading scripture, serving communion, and ushering. Susia participates in book and Bible studies, and we have served on committees and the church council. Our shared Christian values influence many aspects of our life. Each December, we give away ten percent of our annual income to charity. We support many organizations that have been a part of our family's lives, including the American Cancer Society, the Girl Scouts, and Big Brothers & Big Sisters.

This lovely paragraph shows a family whose church is central to their lives, but that they also treat with some good humor (making faces at the nephews). It paints a vivid picture of their lives as Lutherans (no assumption that we know what that is), and ties in their volunteer efforts as well.

Lev and I were both raised in the Jewish religion, and are very active in our congregation. Our friends there totally support our desire to start a family through adoption and can't wait for our

A minority religion presented in a way that makes it feel immediately safe and welcoming.

(more)

(cont.)
child to become part of the com-
munity. We are spiritually
grounded people and plan to teach
our child high morals and values
in a loving and safe home, with
two committed and responsible
parents.

Hobbies

The word "hobbies" always conjures up for me the activities of 12-year-old boys, like collecting stamps or tracing star constellations. For our purposes, though, hobbies refer to everything you do when you're not at work or being domestic. They can be as complicated at mountain climbing and playing musical spoons, or as simple as reading a book and walking on the beach.

Talking about this part of your life gives you a chance to let a birthmother in on the things that feed your mind, body, and soul. Interpret this section broadly. Expand your thinking about what constitutes a hobby. They could include sports or physical activities, cultural interests (going to the theatre, jazz music), arts or crafts (pottery, making model airplanes), collections (teacups, stamps), tinkering (working on cars, upgrading your computer), or even just areas of interest (WWII airplanes, miniature dollhouses).

Avoid simply listing your activities. Lists are dull and do little to distinguish you from the millions of other people who also hike, bowl, paint, ride bicycles, etc. Describe what you do, but also write about why you do it. Give your reader a glimpse into what these activities mean to you and you'll open up a whole side of yourself they may not have seen before. It's a great opportunity to paint pictures of what you have to offer a child (presumably, your kid will be exposed to these interests as well). It's also a prime place to demonstrate how a child will fit into your life.

➤ **Here are some examples:**

I like being a "handyman" and I keep busy building things like bookcases or a rose trellis for our climbing roses. Working with my hands, seeing something built right, gives me a great feeling that all is right with the world, and I look forward to having a "little shadow" ask me what I am doing so I can show our youngster how things work. We enjoy gardening and want to share the joy of planting things with our kids, to grow a giant pumpkin or see how high a sunflower will reach.

Two simple activities illustrated with richness and detail, each with an eye to how kids will become a part of the family. Much better than a list of twenty activities with no explanation.

We're very adventurous and love to travel (however, we stay clear of tourist areas). We especially loved our visits to Europe and the South Pacific. We dream of traveling with our child, sharing the experience of different cultures and customs, and seeing the world as a family. We love being outdoors.

Admittedly, a very idyllic lifestyle, but it's rendered in an unpretentious manner and with great a clarity that makes you feel like you're there, too.

(more)

(cont.)

When it's warm and sunny, we sail to Catalina Island for the weekend (and we usually see magnificent schools of dolphins on the trip over). We find a quiet cove, hike, and picnic on the island during the day, and barbecue, read, and enjoy the beautiful sunsets on the boat at night. We often talk about how amazing it will be to share these sailing trips with our child.

We spend many of our after-work hours around the house, taking walks (even in the snow), unwinding in front of the TV, and hanging out with our 2 playful house rabbits (litterbox-trained, by the way). On the weekends we enjoy visiting friends or family, finding new places to go or just puttering around the house. We are not overly interested in buying luxury items — instead we prefer to go places or do things that give us memories and stories to share with others. We often take short trips to places where we haven't

This communicates a very unique point of view, with nice details. I'd like to see an anecdote added so that it moves from being an idea to being something you can picture.

(more)

(cont.)

been to see the wildlife, nature, and scenery. We feel that trying new activities both at home & while traveling is a great learning and eye-opening experience.

We grow a lot of herbs and vegetables in our garden and Siobhan loves spending time creating nice dishes in her kitchen from our freshly picked produce. Cooking & needlework are two of her favorite hobbies, so not only is our house filled with many of her creations but it also smells wonderful around dinnertime every evening. I love to garden, and I've done quite a bit of work with the yard. We have roses and flowers of almost every color all year round, although we especially love summer when the sunflowers are in full bloom. I've already staked out a small plot for our first child to plant when they're old enough (although you're never too young to get your thumbs green!).

Again, simple and specific.

Birthmother Support

The law in most states allows potential adoptive parents to provide financial support to the birthmother, often with the stipulation that it is for reimbursement of expenses incurred during the pregnancy and relating to the health and welfare of the child. But the whole subject of birthmother support is a controversial one within the adoption community, not because some birthmothers rightly need financial assistance to see their babies born healthy and happy, but because the moment you introduce money into a relationship as intimate and personal as this, you open the possibility that it will become corrupted.

For instance, if a birthmother needs help getting to and from her doctor's appointment, is it appropriate to reimburse her cab fare, or buy her a car? Everyone draws that ethical line differently, and differently for each situation. Despite the sensationalized media view, there is little "baby buying" going on in the U.S., but abuses of the good intent of the law do occur, on both the potential adoptive parent and birthmother sides of the equation.

Some adoption professionals do recommend that you mention your ability to support the birthmother during the pregnancy with a benign phrase like, "We will be happy to contribute to your support to the extent the law allows." Some oppose any up-front mention of it. Have a frank conversation with your advisor to see where s/he stands.

My thinking goes like this (and I am speaking personally here): The idea of a Dear Birthmother letter is to attract a birthmother who is right for you. If you make money a central part of your outreach, you are likely to attract birthmothers for whom money is central to their decision to place. If you are comfortable with that type of relationship, and the complexities and values it brings, then you should feel free to put it out there.

If, like my wife and I do, you feel strongly that your birthmother relationship should be built on human concerns rather than mercantile ones, then make those values central to your letter, and deal with any necessary financial considerations later through your adoption professional.

Closing Paragraphs

Close your letter with a final thought, a wish for your birthmother, and a hug. It's a good place to reinforce your respect for her decision-making process as well.

Keep it simple, it's not a tearful good-bye. Quite the contrary, it's an invitation to further contact. Let your last words be upbeat and positive. **Make sure you list your contact information again at the end of your letter.**

MAKING YOUR LETTER TERRIFIC

A Dear Birthmother letter, by its very nature, is a difficult sort of piece to write. It is inherently passive, descriptive, and historical, yet its goals are exactly the opposite: to engage, involve, and connect.

Now that you understand the form, style, and content of a good Dear Birthmother letter, it's time to focus on the qualities that separate terrific letters from merely adequate ones. The big idea that runs through all four of these principles is simple, but powerful: **Be specific.** You will vastly improve your ability to connect to the right birthmother if you create clear, indelible images for her to visualize and remember.

Paint Pictures

A university professor, speaking to his students about her disappointment in their work, once said, "We sent you, our young art-

ists, out into the desert to tell us what was there. You returned and
told us how you felt. And we never saw the desert." In journalism,
we call this idea, "Show, don't tell," and it's a hard lesson to learn.

People think in images, not ideas. Good writing is vivid writing, writing that conjures pictures in the reader's mind and gives
them a firsthand experience of the desert, just as if they had visited
for themselves its wind-rippled, caramel dunes. The more clearly
you employ details that spur the reader's imagination, the more in-
delibly your writing will impress them.

> **Here's an example:**

The view from our house is unbelievable.

This statement says nothing to a birthmother except that you
like your view. It tells how you feel about it, but shows them no
clear picture of what you are talking about. In turn, they learn nothing about who you are. Compare it with this:

*In the summer, we often sit together on our old oak bench and
watch the sunset against the Allegheny Mountains. The golden
light on the jagged peaks just takes our breath away.*

This helps a birthmother visualize both the view *and* you enjoying the view. In this way, you describe your home and reveal something of yourself in a single stroke. You don't have to be a poet to
write this way, just take the extra moment to make the experience
real–the type of bench, the color of the light, the character of the
mountains. Write what you see, hear, taste, touch, and smell. **Show,
don't tell.** Images evoke feeling in others.

Illuminate with Anecdotes

Share your stories with your readers. It makes them feel included and makes your life more tangible to them. Anecdotes provide the kind of specific personal details that help birthmothers form pictures of the life their child might enjoy.

➤ **Here's an example:**

Our wedding day was very special to us.

This statement shares nothing, and gives nothing for the reader to visualize and remember. Again, it tells us how you felt about the event and shows us nothing of the day. Worse, it's too general, and gives your reader nothing to distinguish you from anyone else. Every wedding day is special, even those that lead to divorce.

On our wedding day, we made our own floral arrangements of purple bearded irises and violets (my favorites). Later, John got a little wild while dancing and knocked over a large vase of them. Not only did I marry the man of my dreams, but also I watched him rolling around in a slippery mass of purple flowers wearing a white tux. We both laughed for days.

This is a story a reader can picture, and one she won't soon forget. It also brings her into the moment and allows her to share this memory with you. Share your stories, those simple little moments you tell repeatedly to your friends. They humanize you. **The more generous you are with the specifics of your life, the more included a birthmother will feel.**

Fit the Child Into Your Life

Whenever possible, use the description of your interests, job, home, and any other plain fact as an opportunity to talk about parenting and how you will raise your child. **Never lose sight of the fact that a birthmother is reading your letter trying to imagine what their baby's life will be like.** Your goal is to help her see it. The more specific the details you provide, the deeper and more lasting the impression you will make.

If you're waiting to adopt your first child, your life probably looks fairly adult—dinner parties, bowling leagues, movies, work, the theatre—many activities that don't seem to easily accommodate a baby. You must communicate these interests in order to paint a picture of who you are, but also look for ways to describe how a child will fit in. If you love to go to the theatre, for instance, describe how you plan to introduce this passion to your children by taking them to puppet shows and children's musicals, like your parents did you. If golf is your thing, make a joke about needing a caddie and how much fun it will be for baby to drive the cart. Help a birthmother picture her child participating in your life, even if she hates golf or has never been to the theatre.

As an aside, it always seems specious to me when I read about active, intelligent adults who say they are going to drop everything of interest and become Pooh-parents, full of lullabies and googly love. I don't buy it. Sure, many of us do become this way around babies, but your Dear Birthmother letter should strive to encompass the totality of your child's developing years, not just the goo-goo time. You won't be singing lullabies when s/he leaves for college (and if you do, s/he certainly won't be speaking to you any more). Paint a picture of who you are now, as well as who you hope to become when you are a family.

Explain Your References

If something is meaningful to you, find the clear, specific language to communicate the reasons why. Your goal is to cast as wide a net as possible. To do so, you must include birthmothers who may not share or appreciate your experiences the way you do.

➤ **For example:**

We love the yearly slaughter here on the farm.

Just because it seems plainly obvious to you that there is nothing in the world more emotionally moving than butchering the hogs each fall, you shouldn't necessarily assume that everyone shares your porcine zeal. A statement like this is too vague and will likely lead to misunderstanding. Take the time to explain what the yearly slaughter means to you and what you think it teaches a child. You might still be passed over by a birthmother who is a vegetarian, or who thinks hog butchering is simply gross, but you might be contacted by one who has simply never visited a farm or experienced the beauty and the majesty of its circle of life. She'll respect you because you shared your passion in a way she could understand.

This applies equally to hobbies, jobs, family situations, and even religion. Your belief in Christ, or Allah, or Buddha, or Jehovah, or Isis is very specific to you. To say simply, "We believe in Yoda" communicates very little to a birthmother who might have a very different personal spiritual background or who has never seen Star Wars. To one person, saying "I'm a Jew" means that you pray three times a day and wear a black hat; to someone else, it means that you like lox and bagels on Sunday morning. Similarly, "we are Christian" could mean that you believe in the literal word of Christ as a guiding principle of your every waking day, or merely that your parents baptized you when you were born and you sometimes go to church bake sales.

Explain your references not in the way a teacher explains to a student who doesn't understand, but rather from the generous feeling of wanting to share yourself with another person. It's a key step in painting a full and specific portrait of your life.

A FEW PET PEEVES

A Word on Need

This is probably one of the most difficult things to discuss about Dear Birthmother letters, and perhaps the most difficult thing to understand. But if there is nothing else you take away from this book, take this.

Infertility sucks, and it can beat the crap out of a person's self-esteem. After years of trying, and imagining, and hoping, the desire to have a child can sometimes seem so powerful that need alone seems enough to bring a baby into your life.

But I feel strongly that birthmothers really don't care about potential adoptive parents' problems, or their need. They have enough on their minds. They are dealing with the Big Problem—an unplanned pregnancy—and I think the last thing most of them want is to get involved with someone whose neediness is going to make further emotional demands on them.

Expressing excessive need also does very little to distinguish you from all the other people looking for a child. Think about it for a moment: every potential adoptive parent wants a baby. Unfortunately, babies don't go to people just because they want them the most. Personally, many birthmothers to whom my wife and I spoke expressed to us that one of the reasons they responded to our letter was that so many of the other letters sounded so desperate.

There is a moment in a Dear Birthmother letter for you to make a heartfelt and emotionally honest statement about how much you want a child, and you should find it and make the most of it. But all the rest is about sharing the joy of who you are and the life you lead.

Here's another perspective. A birthmother counselor I spoke with said that she thinks that, in fact, birthmothers have an acute sense of your pain; they can easily relate to feelings of loss. But this counselor feels just as strongly, as I do, that you shouldn't burden them with your anguish, needs, or problems. To do so engages a birthmother in a relationship based on guilt; she wants to help you because she feels badly for you. If later in the relationship, she develops concerns or fears, this guilt can prevent her from honestly confiding them for fear of causing you more hurt. When communication isn't free, pressure builds up, people feel trapped, and, sometimes, otherwise preventable explosions and last-minute changes of heart result.

I suggest that you reach out to your birthmother in love and generosity. Communicate support for her, awareness of her concerns, and an easygoing, reassuring attitude. Send the message that working with you will be an emotionally positive, safe, and birthmother-centered experience. In the end, you will find your letter expresses the geography of your heart in a much more substantial and inviting way.

That all being said, there are certainly some birthmothers attracted to guilt and need. If need is the overwhelming central note of your life, you should ignore what I say, and do what you think best. Need is a little like money in this way: if it's central to your letter than it will likely be central to the birthmother who chooses you. If you are comfortable with it being the currency of your relationship, sing it out as loudly and clearly as you can. As always, be who you are and let your letter reflect that.

A Gush about Gush

A word here about what I call "gush," but what some might think of as overly sentimentalized speech or excessive cuteness.

There is a school of thought among some adoption professionals that the best way to appeal to a birthmother is to speak to her "on her level." They base this recommendation on the thought that the "typical" birthmother is a young, silly girl, easily duped by cheap emotional appeals. They recommend a whole range of infantilizing actions, such as potential adoptive mothers renaming themselves with "cute" diminutives (Patti for Patricia, Chrissi for Christine, Susie for Susan–and can you dot your "i" with a flower?). They suggest that you fill your letter with references to tummy mommies, butterfly kisses, teddy bears, and other childish sentimentality. Frequently there is the not-so-subtle suggestion that there is some sort of attractiveness to be achieved by covering your letter with those heart-shaped stickers favored by high school girls.

I have problems with this approach on a number of levels: 1) It's horribly condescending to a person who is in the process of making one of the most important decisions of her life, 2) It makes an often erroneous assumption about who is the "typical" birthmother, and 3) It's riddled with banal cliches.

Clearly, having read this far in the book, you know I believe that authenticity and honesty are the two most important hallmarks of a successful Dear Birthmother letter. Don't misunderstand me here, I have nothing against butterfly kisses if that's a part of who you are (they are quite nice, actually, and I recommend them highly). What I object to, and strenuously, is false sentimentality, the kind of fake cutesiness that represents a cheap attempt to manipulate emotions.

If rhyming poetry says something essential about who you are, I'm all for it, no matter how sentimental it might be. But don't manufacture it. Express what's in your heart—your silliness and your love—but do it honestly. Don't get all goo-goo because someone told you it's a good way to "catch" a birthmother. The only thing you'll catch is a world of headaches when the birthmothers who finally choose you share nothing of your true outlook on life.

We are All Blessed

Avoid excessive use of such "humble" phrases such as "We are blessed to…" "We are lucky to… or "We have been fortunate to…." You may think you are softening the sense that you are tooting your own horn, but in fact, the effect is just the opposite. Qualifying everything in this way makes you seem insecure, or worse, insincerely humble.

Don't waste time telling birthmothers how you feel about your life. Put it out there, simply and honestly, and let them decide how fortunate, lucky, or blessed you are.

On Points!

As a side note, please be judicious in your use (and abuse!) of exclamation points! As one adoption lawyer said to me, any paragraph with more than one exclamation point is just wrong!! And I think he's being generous!!! Exclamation points make you seem breathless! And panicky! And mostly, people just hate that!!!!!

Express your enthusiasm through your vivid writing, careful attention to detail, and open heart. Sans exclamation points, please.

THE WRITING PROCESS

This moment–sitting down and writing the thing–conjures for many their worst nightmares. Suddenly, the ghost of their third grade English teacher arises and goes screaming down the hall waving a grammar book in one hand and a dangling participle in the other. It's enough to make grown-ups run sniveling for the cloakroom.

Don't worry. I haven't taken you this far only to abandon you at the precipice. True, this book cannot make you a great writer. But you don't need to be a great writer to write a great Dear Birthmother letter. It's far more important to write truly from the heart, something anyone can do, than to parade your vocabulary and twist a witty line. But good writing does make for good reading, and one of your goals is to create a letter that is lively, inviting, and easy to read. This chapter deals with the writing process itself.

Some of you will feel comfortable just sitting down and writing, working on your letter in the way that's natural and comfortable to you. For you, this chapter offers some fresh ideas for revising and editing that you may find helpful

If the idea of putting pen to paper (or electron to word processor) makes you wish you could have a root canal instead, this chapter provides the tools to get through this process with a minimum of pain, and perhaps a bit of fun. Its systematic approach makes even the most mundane writing active, more accessible, and more enjoyable to read.

The Step-by-Step Approach

Because of it's relatively short length, you can write a Dear Birthmother letter incrementally, step-by-step. This eight-step approach outlines one possible way.

You can likewise revise it through a series of editorial "passes," each of which attempts to improve a single aspect of the writing. Following the writing steps, you'll find seven suggestions to manage the revision process. Recall the first tip at the beginning of this book: *writing begins with rewriting*. Knowing the revision steps in advance should free you of the need to be brilliant with every stroke of your pen.

Step One: Write freely

No matter which of the two of you will be responsible for the final document, I suggest that each spouse begin on their own. Don't consult beforehand. Just write and see what you each come up with. You may be pleasantly surprised by what your spouse contributes, and it may spark new ideas in you.

Think of this first step as a jam session. Free yourself from the pressure to begin at the beginning or to proceed in an orderly fashion. Jot down ideas as they come to you. Write a true sentence that comes from your heart. Babble on for pages about your home or your job.

Free yourself from the responsibility to write neat, well-constructed paragraphs with a beginning, middle, and end. Don't censor yourself. Write short, write long, write any way you can, but write! You've got to get stuff down on paper so you have the raw material with which to work.

Step Two: If the words aren't coming, make lists

Lists are great. They get ideas on paper and you don't even have to write full sentences. Just jot notes. Here are some ideas, but you should make up your own:

➢ *My hobbies, and why I love them*

➢ *Things we love to do together*

➢ *Reasons my job is great*

➢ *Five things I most want to teach my child*

➢ *The three best things my parents ever did for me*

➢ *What I love about my spouse*

➢ *The best Sundays of our marriage*

➢ *What grandma plans to do for the baby*

➢ *Three personal stories that tell you a lot about me*

Step Three: Compare notes

Together, cull through what you've written individually and find the sentences that really speak the truth. Discuss together what you like and what doesn't resonate, and why. Take notes as you do.

Pull out the good stuff and build around it. Add details, anecdotes, and other related ideas that come to mind. Lose all the excess stuff that seems off-point or nonessential.

Step Four: Organize sections

Look at the material you have and see what form it seems to suggest. Is the best stuff of the he says/she says variety? Does it seem to be subject oriented? Begin to separate the material that seems related into sections that make sense.

Choose a voice to write in. Perhaps it's clear from what you already have written, perhaps not. Try to think of the way you would best want this story told to you—by someone you know? Someone objective? The person whom it is about? In a song? A poem? Don't be afraid to think outside the box. Find a form and voice that seems natural to you.

Step Five: Build paragraphs

Working one section at a time, begin to build paragraphs around each central idea. They need not be long; four or five sentences is plenty. Add in the facts and images that make each subject seem concrete to you. Don't worry about the quality of the writing yet; focus on the content.

Show, don't tell. Add details that you can see, hear, touch, taste, and smell. Think in pictures. Then add anecdotes and personal stories.

Step Six: Prioritize

Arrange your sections in order of importance to you. It doesn't matter what form you are working in, put the most important stuff first. Look at what results. Are there pieces that seem to be missing? Add any sections that you feel should belong.

Step Seven: Write for Flow

Put your working document to one side, get a clean sheet of paper, and begin again. Write or copy the letter from beginning to end, using your first document as a guide. The goal here is to write for flow. Connect one idea to the next in a way that seems natural and makes sense to you. Copy liberally from your working document.

This is not a final draft, so don't get bogged down if you run into an awkward patch. Mark it for later and move on. This is an "additive pass." Fill in the connective tissue to flesh out the story.

Step Eight: The Pause that Refreshes

Congratulations! You've just completed your **first draft**.

Now, put it away in a drawer and don't look at it for a week. Let the letter sit so you can return to it with fresh eyes. If you get further ideas, jot them down elsewhere and save them for later.

Use this time to begin selecting photographs.

Revising

Now that you've gotten your first draft together, either in your own fashion or by employing the steps outlined here, you probably have a long text that has some great lines, some bad ones, some paragraphs that meander, and some that are right on point. Now we get on to the tough stuff (made easy).

The reason why most people have trouble revising their work is that when they read it over, it "sounds" pretty good. So, they read it again. Still good. And again. And again. And the more they read it, the more it sounds the same. The problem with this technique is that each reading tries to answer the same question: Does it make sense to me? And the answer is always more or less the same: Of course it makes sense to you, you wrote the dang thing! The question you really need to answer is: "Will it make sense to a reader who doesn't know me, and if it does, will it be so good that it "sings?"

The key to answering this question, and improving your text, is finding ways to distance yourself from it each time you read, to see it with fresh eyes as if you're reading it for the first time. The following editorial passes ask you to read the text with a specific question in mind like, "are all my verbs vibrant and active?" You'll rewrite productively not by fixing everything at once, but rather by focusing on one, narrow task at a time.

Don't be surprised, however, if in the process of a punctuation check you find yourself drastically changing a paragraph that suddenly doesn't sound right. That's exactly the point. Limiting your reading to the task at hand frees up your peripheral vision. With each pass, you will discover things that you didn't catch before, like redundancies you can eliminate, images you can vivify, or sentences you can distill. "Scrubbing" the text in this way helps you systematically eliminate common writing errors while simultaneously enhancing your creativity.

Pass One: General rewrite

Your first pass is just to revisit the material in any way that seems comfortable, and improve it as best you can. Add, cut, change, revise, anything that strikes your fancy. Your one-week layoff should sufficiently refresh your eyes to see the text anew. **The result of this pass will be your revised draft.**

When it's complete, and you feel good about where you are, proceed with the following passes. Aim to do a little each night and spread out the process over a few days. Each time you leave and return to the material, you'll see new ways to improve it.

Pass Two: Verb scrub

In a short letter, you can't afford to waste words that don't add sparkle and vibrancy to your writing. Verbs do more to enliven our language than any other part of speech. Verbs propel good writing, and lend your writing energy, presence, and commitment.

Begin by eliminating as many instances of *to be* and *to have* as you can.

➢ **Here are some examples:**

Weak	Strong
We have been married two years.	We married two years ago.
Florida is where I was raised.	I grew up in Florida.
Our vacation was a trip to Crete.	We vacationed in Crete.
Our commitment to you is to provide a loving, nurturing, and active family.	We promise to provide a loving, nurturing, and active family.

Weak	*Strong*
Marketing was Sylvia's major.	Sylvia majored in marketing.
Our house was filled with yummy smells from Mom's famous roast lamb and fresh baked pie	The yummy smells of Mom's famous roast lamb and fresh baked pie filled our house.
I love seeing the joy on Jim's face when he is playing with our nieces or is teaching them new songs.	I love the joy on George's face when he plays with our nieces or teaches them new songs.

In many of the previous examples, you'll notice the subject of a sentence using *to be* can often be converted to an active verb phrase, like, *Our commitment to you is...* becomes *We promise.*

➤   **Here's a paragraph written by the Wizard of Is:**

Lola is a very creative and sociable child. She is fond of Kindergarten, and her teachers are all reporting that she is doing very well. When she is not in school, she is often enjoying recreational sports such as soccer, bike riding, baseball, and swimming.

➤   **Here it is, well scrubbed:**

A creative and sociable child, Lola loves Kindergarten, where her teachers report she really excels. After school, she plays soccer and baseball, rides bikes, and swims.

While scrubbing out all those occurrences of *is, are, has, have, am,* and *was,* you may discover yourself face to face with sentences that can't do with out them, like *Dave is a customer service manager* or *Vicky has two sisters.* These sentences are fine, but don't be satisfied with too many statements of fact. Does Dave's job provide an opportunity to say something about his character? Could you share something salient about Vicky's sister, other than she exists? How about, *As a customer service manager, Dave loves helping people,* or *Vicky's two sisters can't wait to become aunts.* Don't waste an opportunity to deepen understanding.

Check each verb, verb by verb. Assure that each is vivid and active. Employ a thesaurus to find interesting alternatives to banal verbs. Don't *like* when you can *love, adore,* or *relish.* Don't *go* when you can *travel, journey,* or *visit.* Don't select esoteric language that doesn't seem to you natural and informal, but whenever possible, select verbs that convey enthusiasm, desire, passion, depth of feeling, and an active engagement with the world.

This pass will have a second benefit: it will force you to make active those sentences that are written in the passive voice.

Pass Three: Make it Active

To the best of your ability, write in the active voice. A sentence is in the active voice when the subject does the action the verb describes.

We love *our jobs*

We is the subject; *love* is the action.

The sentence is in the passive voice when the subject is acted upon.

Our jobs are loved *by us.*

Our jobs is the subject; *loved by us* is the action. Thus, *our love* is acting on the subject, *our jobs*. The subject is passive, i.e., doing nothing but existing in a state of being loved.

If this seems confusing, don't worry; you'll get the hang of it. Notice how the passive sentence uses a form of *to be*? Pass Two will help you locate passive sentences.

➤ **Here are some more examples:**

Passive Voice	*Active Voice*
Tradition, love, and a thirst for fun are embraced by our family.	*Our family embraces tradition, love, and a thirst for fun.*
He was hired by his brother.	*His brother hired him.*
A blessing was given to us.	*We received a blessing.*
Your child will be loved and cared for by us.	*We will love and care for your child.*

The passive voice avoids responsibility and suppresses identity, the two things you most want to communicate to a birthmother. You want to show a birthmother that you are people who act on the world, not ones on whom the world acts. Match what you say to how you say it. Always use the active voice.

Pass Four: Speak the Speech

Read your letter out loud. As you do, note any sentence that doesn't come out of your mouth easily or that feels stilted and unnatural. Rewrite it to sound more like natural speech.

Next, read it to someone, and ask him or her to raise their hand if any sentence sounds more like "writing," than talking, or if it doesn't sound like you. Again, rewrite anything that seems stilted. Don't be afraid to use contractions whenever they seem natural.

Not every sentence will work well spoken out loud, but this exercise will help you weed out awkward speech and achieve a friendlier, more informal voice.

Pass Five: Optimize Your Paragraphs

Examine each paragraph for length. None should be longer than four or five sentences. Start a new paragraph whenever the idea changes, the speaker changes, or it seems to make sense. Try different paragraph breaks and see how each affects meaning. Review the example on pages 29-30.

Now check each paragraph to see if it's as compact and essential as it can be. Is there a simpler and more direct way to rephrase something that seems long-winded? You want your prose to be tight, but not so tight that it's laborious to read. Think economy, not compression.

Pass Six: Section Check

Go section by section, or subject by subject, through your text and reread the section of this book dealing with that subject matter. Look at the examples. Does your material achieve all you want it to? Does it seem to express your feelings well?

Pass Seven: Spell Checking

Run your draft through your computer's grammar checker. Grammar checkers will often pick up passive sentences that you missed on your other passes. By forcing you to examine sentences individually, They also provide another opportunity to review your work objectively. Be aware that the grammar checker may flag as incorrect sentences that you intend to be informal, so don't take its word for law.

Finally, run your spell checker. This alone is not enough, however. You must make a careful, word by word examination of your final draft. **Spell checkers can knot all ways find thins that otherwise could bee spelled write.** The best way to find spelling errors is to read each sentence backwards, word by word. This forces you to look at each word devoid of meaning and context. You'll catch misspellings that you missed before.

Again, congratulations! **This is your final draft.** Read it to a couple of close friends who understand your adoption journey and see if they think it's "you." If they don't, get new friends.

Deadlines

Writers love deadlines. They are the only reason we get anything done. This book got finished because I placed an ad in a magazine offering it for sale. If I hadn't bought the ad (and risked humiliation for not finishing on time), I'd still be writing today. (I didn't finish on time, but that's another story.)

Perhaps you are a highly disciplined person, capable of setting your mind to something and getting it done. If so, bully for you. For the rest of us, I highly suggest you sit down with your partner (if you have one), pull out your calendars, and set up some deadlines for completing your letter. Use the following checklist to help you schedule tasks; it works well if you begin on a Monday.

Give yourself no more than one month to complete the entire process, from first draft to final printing. I know this sounds like a long time, but you're a busy person, and it always takes longer than you might expect. Deprive yourself of something you love until you get it done, like no movies, or no pizza–anything will do. This helps make the deadline real. If you cheat—feel guilty. My Jewish mother always said: guilt gets things done.

WRITING STAGES CHECKLIST

Activity	Duration	Due by:
His/her jam *(step 1)*	*5 days*	_____
1st draft *(steps 2-7)*	*7 days*	_____
Pause *(step 8)* (select photos)	*7 days*	_____
Revised draft *(pass 1)*	*2 days*	_____
Scrubbing *(passes 2-8)*	*8 days*	_____
Final proof	*1 day*	_____
Print *(party!)*		_____

SELECTING GREAT PHOTOS

Every Dear Birthmother letter needs at least one photo, preferably more. Speak with your provider and use as many as s/he allows. Nothing communicates intangibles like a good picture can. As one lawyer told me, "If a picture's worth a thousand words, than ten pictures are worth ten-thousand words."

That being said, there are good pictures and bad pictures, and you'd be surprised how many people can't tell the difference. Here are some rules to follow to make sure your pictures speak as clearly as your words.

Pictures of a Life

Select photographs that show a birthmother how you live rather than how you look. Your photos should be meaningful, cheerful, and tell a story about who you are. Don't worry about double chins, bad hair days, or dark circles under your eyes. Don't stress that the pictures show your crowfeet; smiles, smiles, smiles.

Show lots of face. A good photo makes a connection with its audience. It communicates energy, enthusiasm, emotion, action, and accessibility. It makes you smile when you look at it. No photo does that if your face is in profile or hidden behind a palm tree or sunglasses.

Here's a tip: cull your possible photos and then show the best of them to other people, both strangers and friends. Watch their faces as they look at them. A good photo brings a warm smile to people's faces without need for an explanation.

Here are some stories you could be looking to tell:

➢ **We really love each other** – a portrait where you are physically touching one another, looking into each other's eyes, or hugging and making eye contact with the camera.

➢ **Our home is a warm and inviting place** – a picture of the front of your house with an inviting garden in full bloom on a sunny day, a picture of one of you in the kitchen smiling while you lick cake frosting from a beater.

➢ **We're warm and happy people** – a photo of you together doing something silly, throwing pizza dough, playing with dogs, at a carnival or at a picnic.

➢ **We lead an active lifestyle** – a close-up of you together with skis, basketball, scuba equipment, bicycles, hiking equipment, etc. (no pictures of small people on big mountains!).

➤ **We enjoy our time together** – walking on the beach (close-up), reading a book, sitting on a boat, or a swing, or any other quiet place.

➤ **We love kids** – playing with a happy kid, sitting at a computer helping a happy child, carrying a happy kid piggy back, holding a smiling baby, making faces at a stinky diaper. Never use a picture of other people's children as your only picture, and always caption it *(see note about captions)*.

➤ **Our family is close** – portraits of the extended families, lots of smiling people being happy together.

Photo Quality

All images should be in sharp focus. Faces especially should be sharp. Don't use blurry or grainy snaps, or ones with poor contrast. Select photos with lifelike color values. You can use a black-and-white shot if it is superlative and not your only photo. Remember, this is about the subject, not the photo. No art is needed, just great life.

As dumb as this may sound, it must be said: **Use recent photos that look like you.** I know you love that great shot from your Hawaiian vacation ten years ago, but you had a beard then and were twenty-five. A birthmother is going to want to meet you eventually, and when she shows up at the restaurant, you want her to recognize you immediately and smile, not feel she's been set up on a disappointing blind date.

Subject-to-Background Ratio

Select photographs where the subject takes up at least $4/5^{ths}$ of the frame. There's almost nothing worse than a 3" x 3" photo of the two of you hugging at the Grand Canyon, where you are 1/2" tall and the Canyon takes up the rest of the photo. Respectfully, no birthmother wants the Grand Canyon to adopt her baby. Photos where vistas, lakes, mountains, artwork, or any other background element takes up more room than people in the foreground should be left in the album.

Lighting

Select photos where your faces are well and evenly lit. Photos taken in bright sunlight tend to leave eye sockets in deep shadow, and eyes are the mirrors to the soul (or something like that).

Likewise, photos whose background is much brighter than you in the foreground will make your faces seem dark and drawn. Don't use pictures where you suffer from "red eye," unless you are a vampire (although red eye can be easily fixed either digitally or with a special pen available at most photo finishers).

Candid, Not Studio

If you can, avoid studio pictures or pictures in which you look overly posed. Avoid photos where you're dressed formally, no matter how great you looked in that tux or ballgown. You want formality to be seen as an aspect of your life, not the dominant note. I think it's safe to say that few birthmothers are interested in a family where Junior must come to dinner each night in his little tux.

If you must use a studio shot, never use more than one, and immediately contrast it with one that is candid, spontaneous, and above all, casual

I'm not a big fan of wedding pictures, either. Face it, none of us look anything like what we looked like on our wedding day. Weddings are a time apart from the real world. Birthmothers don't care what you looked like on your most beautiful day; they want to know what you look like everyday. Save the wedding album for when a birthmother comes to visit you.

Pets

Pets are like members of the family, so close-up pictures of your expressive, cuddly, and happy animals are great. Pictures of you at play with your pets are even better.

If your pets are scary-looking (pit bulls, ferrets, pythons), think twice.

Captions

Captions provide another opportunity to add to your story. Write captions for photos that need or benefit from explanation. Avoid them when the situation is obvious, like "Patrick and Susan kissing."

Always caption clearly pictures that include other people's children. A birthmother will *immediately* assume that any children pictured are yours. If she specifically wants a child-free couple, she may quickly turn the page. For this reason, never make a picture of you with other people's children the only picture you present.

Great captions inform, but also extend your story. Show a little personality. Sometimes a caption can expand on something that's not obvious, encouraging the reader to examine the picture more closely to catch a nuance. Even without pictures, the following sample captions allow you to imagine what's being pictured. Try to write interesting captions that similarly reveal.

> ## ➤ Here are some examples

Italy is a great place to kiss.

Fred and Nina (our best friend's daughter) love to share secrets.

Fluffy appointed herself Queen of the House. We are her loyal subjects.

June planted the rose garden the week we moved in.

There's no place like home, except when a pipe bursts.

LAYOUT & DESIGN

It's often at this stage of the process that the issues many of us feel surrounding "advertising for babies" come into sharpest focus. As a culture, we are so accustomed to seeing slick, professional design in everything from TV ads to personal correspondence that it's very easy to get caught up valuing form over content. We know that birthmothers live in the same world, and see the same images everyday; it would be naive to think that they are less visually sophisticated than we are.

Always keep in mind that the essence of this communication is personal, not mercantile. You've worked your butt off to write a letter that really reflects who you are; stick to your guns and find a design that does so too. You need not live up to the standards of professional advertising, and one might argue that you shouldn't. If, for example, typing your letter on lined notebook paper and pasting on it a color photo or two matches your personal aesthetic, then go for it. You will be making a strong statement. Likewise, if graphic arts are your thing, then you should go for that as well.

You want to demonstrate the same care in the letter's presentation that you showed in its creation. Personally, I think some middle ground is called for–well-produced enough for it to look like you took some care in its doing, but not so slick that it seems like a sales brochure or a come-on.

Being a writer, not a designer, I can't give you an in-depth tutorial on graphic design. But I can share some general tips and bugaboos that adoption professionals have noticed over the years either work, or don't. I suggest you have a quick conversation with your adoption professional and ask him or her to share his or her thoughts. Also, ask for examples of letters s/he believes work well.

Keep it Clean

Graphic design acts like the frame of a painting. Done well, it complements and enhances the image; done poorly, it draws attention from it. The goal of good design is readability.

When design becomes decoration for decoration's sake, you've gone too far. Avoid unnecessary clutter on the page. Use a simple, presentable font for the main text, the same or an even simpler one for captions, and perhaps another (more decorative if you prefer) for subheads. Never use more than three fonts in a document; two is preferred.

If you choose to break up the text in columns, keep them large enough to be easily readable. If you lay out the text in a block, say, around a photograph, try to keep sections together. Roaming around the page to follow the narrative can be confusing and difficult.

Don't clutter the page with excessive graphics–like hearts, or stars, or teddy bears–either with stickers or computer graphics. If you would like to employ a graphic motif, keep it simple and elegant, like the three-leaf graphic used in this book.

Avoid Gray Pages

Remember *gray pages* from our discussion of subheads? In addition to typographical variation, the easiest way to break up a gray page is with a picture or two. Wrap the text around it, like I've done with this paragraph and the graphic to the right. I do not recommend you insert meaningless graphics into your letter, as I've done here by way of example, but you can do the same thing with a photograph. Place a couple of color photos on a page, say upper right and lower left, to give the page a nice visual flow. More will tend to feel cluttered. It's rather simple to do on a computer, and if you don't have one, you can always revert to the tried and true method of printing out your text with smaller margins and pasting it on the page next to a photo. Use a color photocopier to copy the results and no one will be the wiser.

Finish Simply

Your final letter will need to contain color photos, and some adoption professionals recommend that you paste photo reprints directly on to the document. This can become a complicated and costly exercise, especially if you are planning on making a large number of copies to distribute to your friends-and-family network. If you can't create pages with photos in your computer, I suggest you paste up a master version and color copy it. It will save you lots of time and many sticky fingers.

Unless your professional presents letters to birthmothers in a specific way, a simple staple will bind your final document very well. There is no need for costly binders or report covers. Some providers will advocate extensive arts projects, with pictures and text intricately pasted on special papers. This approach is fine if you have the time and inclination, but hardly seems necessary. This is about you, not about office supplies. Keep it simple. The important thing here is the message.

CONCLUSION

In this case, the end is a beginning, both for your letter and for your journey to parenthood. The wonderful, heartening thing about adoption is that if you stick to it, you will become parents. The road is not always easy (although sometimes it is), nor short (although it can be that, too), but it is always fulfilling.

A couple of weeks after our son, Charlie, was born, my wife picked her head up from whatever dirty diaper she was managing and mentioned that, after nearly five years of trying to have a family (four years of infertility and one on the adoption path), it seemed like no time had passed at all. The concerns of Charlie's present had wiped away the tribulations of our past. I paused a moment, and had to agree. During our worst moments, it was if we were living in some sort of transparent membrane that sealed us off from the rest of the world. Now that we had permeated it, it was as if it never existed.

Don't misunderstand me, we are not the same people we were five years ago. Felling the dragon of infertility tested the limits of our personal resources, but left us with stronger spirits and larger hearts. We know exactly how precious is the miracle of Charlie.

But in my lighter moments (of which there are many these days), I've come to think of our journey as a long detour, as if we'd taken a wrong turn and stumbled into some sort of Buddhist version of purgatory. Once there, a very wise and ancient monk needed to decide the kind of family we would become, and it just took him a bit of time to get it right. Because to Buddhists, you know, slowness is a virtue.

I'm glad he took his time, because the rewards now seem endless.

I wish you the very best in your journey to family, and hope that this humble text makes a small contribution to your eventual success.

Now, go write.

ABOUT THE AUTHOR

Nelson Handel is a journalist and media professional whose print work has appeared in *Family Circle, Bon Appétit, Los Angeles Times Magazine, Adoptive Families, This Old House Magazine, Yahoo Internet Life, Los Angeles Magazine, Offspring, Fine Gardening, Troika,* and many others.

A parent by adoption, he lives in Los Angeles with his wife, Elicia, and their son, Charlie.

APPENDIX 1: LOVE FOR SALE

An essay by the author, reprinted from

ADOPTIVE
FAMILIES
MAGAZINE
Sept./Oct. 2001

A n ad. A brochure. A come-on. A notice of product available for transaction, trade, sale. A product. A commodity. Like a used car that's slightly dinged up, a little older than others, perhaps, but otherwise in fine shape.

Ads are appropriate for used cars. But what should you call it when the merchandise on the block is the willingness of your heart? What do you write when what's at stake is the creation of your family?

Let me backtrack.

My wife and I wanted to have a child. But after four fruitless years in the gristmill of infertility treatments (drugs, inseminations, in vitros, donor eggs), after exhausting our resources (physical, emotional, financial), after burying the monthly hope that our bodies would bring forth children, we accepted the fact that we are infertile. Biology has been quietly put to rest, a haunting memory.

But we still wanted to be parents. We always saw having a family as the next great adventure. So, we turned toward adoption, and as our hearts and spirits began to thaw, adoption filled us with new hope, a sense of possibility we thought still frozen and extinct. We'll be Mommy and Daddy soon, we told ourselves, just one more gauntlet to run.

After examining our options, we decided to pursue an "open" adoption. We liked the idea of connecting with our birthmother, of having her choose us to parent her child, and of choosing her in return. To find prospective parents, we learned, birthmothers contact agencies or adoption attorneys, answer classified ads in Sunday newspapers, and, sometimes, surf the Web. Soon they find themselves reviewing what are known as "dear birthmother" (DBM) letters, documents that introduce the adopting couple and explain why they want to adopt. From these, birthmothers narrow their choices.

So we needed to write one, a DBM letter. Quite suddenly, we found ourselves trying to sell ourselves as parents and, just as quickly, realizing the impossibility of the task. Consider for a moment. If I asked you to tell me, with some measure of certainty, what your life will look like in five years, could you do it? Ten years? Eighteen? Will you still be married? Employed in the same profession? Living under similar circumstances? And how will you raise your child? Can you articulate a cogent philosophy governing the stages of life to come? Nanny, day care, or stay-at-home parent? Private school or public? When asked, who can truly predict more than their intention to live, love, thrive, and grow old in the most positive circumstances they can muster? This letter should be simple, right? "We're nice people and we'll do our best. What more can you ask?" Lots, it turns out.

In the early days of open adoption, DBM letters were single-page biographies. But the competition, if you can call it that, has heated up, and the number of prospective parents has grown enormously. For every healthy newborn available, there are now almost forty potential parents searching. Every type of family you can imagine—married, unmarried, and same-sex couples, single women and single men. It seems like everyone wants a baby.

Suddenly, gray pages of typewritten words look dull. After all, birthmothers live in the same media-saturated world as the rest of us. You have to stand out from the crowd, garner attention, make your pitch.

At first, people enlivened their presentations with a color photo or two. Things quickly escalated. With advances in computer power, digital photography, scanners, and low-cost color printers, these once-simple texts matured (some might say mutated) into well-designed, full-color presentations, corporate prospectuses for WeBeGoodParents Inc.

We were seduced. Both my wife and I have worked in TV advertising, so the process of communicating commercial messages is in our blood. This letter would be our brochure, the come-on to invest in Handels.com. People would buy or pass based on the image we projected, and we resolved to project the best.

We studied letters written by other couples and analyzed their approaches. How were they targeting the market? We coldly analyzed the "competition" and attempted to position ourselves in the field, capitalizing on our strengths (education, humor, compassion) and smoothing over our weaknesses (Los Angeles, working mom, forty years old).

We honed our pitch to the perceived interests of the consumer pool, and tried to be all things to all people. Could we be fun yet firm, stable yet fluid, Caucasian yet multicultural, urban but safe, Jewish yet Christian? How could we translate the left-coastal lifestyle of a couple of former artists into an archetypal American home? We're urban cynics, but the sample letters were lush with what we termed Goo-Goo. Fill your letter with teddy bears, snuggles, and references to "tummy mommies," the Goo-Goo school suggested. Be as cute and cuddly as you can; birthmothers are suckers for this. We found it condescending, but to be safe, we spread on some Goo too.

Then we chose pictures. Days digging through boxes. My nose? Her hair? What says "great parents" to you? Do we look happy or forced? Approachable or remote? Which picture makes our little house look largest? We even spent a day playing with our best friend's kids, taking cutesy pictures. Would they help a birthmother imagine us with children? We considered the subliminal elements and chose a cover photo where our arms formed a heart.

Without really thinking, we ran helter-skelter toward a picture of idealized parents that we believed every birthmother craved. We got high on a sugar rush of pop culture stereotypes, the sweetness of achieving something to overpower the bitter taste of reproductive failure. We would do whatever it took. We could succeed. We would succeed. We must succeed. We...

...stopped. And took a deep breath.

Our hearts were screaming like sprinters' nearing the line, but we had been moving too fast to hear them. This wasn't right. We knew that.

The wonderful thing about writing is that the page becomes a mirror. As you fill it, it reflects all your imperfections, faults, and foibles. Our first drafts showed us an insincerity born of trying to win a game that had beaten us for too many years. We had been infected by the culture; our desire to parent had been transformed into something mercantile. This wasn't how we would find our child, the one who belongs with us, the one whose family we were meant to be. We were disgusted with ourselves and with the whole proposition.

Suddenly those sample letters we'd read so critically shone with different light. Our hearts went out to the couples just like us, struggling desperately to articulate their innermost yearnings. It wasn't a competition; it was kinship. And the birthmothers, we learned, weren't the indigent teens we had stereotyped, but were of diverse ages, differing education, and varied circumstances. Women who, perhaps in the same sure way we knew we wanted to parent a child, knew, that at this moment, they did not.

We began again. We set out to communicate something authentic, some essential measure of truth about how we are in the world and what we might bring to the life of a child. We tried to put into words our love and longing, our deep, primal desire to raise a family, to witness the growth and flowering of a young person and share in his or her life. We embraced anew this imperfect process and struggled to say simply what we desperately felt. We wrote the truth as best we could. In this way, we felt, we would connect with the child we are meant to have. If we weren't perfect people, well then, so be it. Some openhearted woman would see us for who we are and entrust her child's care to our strong circle of love.

But in a culture intoxicated by BabyGap and JonBenet, is it possible to communicate anything as simply held and deeply felt as the urge to parent? Despite our best intentions, our artless letter was columniated and paginated, colored, photo-retouched, and lasered. It had to, or it wouldn't look real sitting in our attorney's stack next to sixty others.

As we handed him the final version, we thought perhaps the medium is no longer the message. If it were, our dear birthmother letter would be as unadorned as our hearts' desire. Instead, our message ended up carefully produced to appear as authentic as it is. Though the truth is naked, its messenger went forth clothed in the emperor's finest.

Postscript:

After finishing the letter, we paid a fee to have it listed among hundreds of others online in an internet registry. It proved to be the right place for us. Our birthmother, who said she read more than 100 letters online before calling us, told us she liked our sense of humor, our quirky lack of convention, and our honesty. As we got to know her, we grew to love the same things about her, too. Our son, Charlie, was born on May 8, 2001. We were there for the birth, and there were lots of smiles, hugs, laughter, and just a few tears of joy to welcome him into the world.

APPENDIX 2:
THE AUTHOR'S
DEAR BIRTHMOTHER LETTER

It's only fair to include my own work for you to evaluate. My wife and I drafted our letter in May 2000 for placement with our adoption attorney. I've learned a lot about adoption since then, and a lot about Dear Birthmother letters.

Just the text is included here; to view the fully formatted final version described in the preceding essay–complete with photos– please visit my web site at www.DearBirthmotherLetter.com/letter. There you will find both the print layout, and the redesigned online version. Same material–different designs.

For a note on the Two-Voice style, see page 45.

Hi, and thanks for reading our letter!

You're looking for a wonderful home for your baby, and we're looking to open our home and family to a new life. *We laugh a lot, and revel in the joy and silliness that life can bring. Over the eleven years we've been together (married for six), we've had lots of good times, and built ourselves a home full of love.* We've overcome personal challenges together, like infertility, and it's made us stronger as individuals and as a couple. We've built a deep respect and lasting love for each other. *We'll raise our children with that respect and love, and with an eye toward developing their individuality and helping them achieve their fullest potential.* We'll fill their lives with warmth, security, and plenty of fun, too.

We know that there's no one exactly like you. You are unique, individual, and blessed with a very special gift to give: the gift of life. Like you, we have a gift to give too. **We have a huge open place in our hearts, waiting for a child to fill it.**

We have the greatest respect for you, and the adoption plan you're making for your baby. *We look forward to meeting with you, and would be happy to keep in touch over the years.* Your baby will always understand how much care and loving consideration you gave in placing him or her for adoption. **As you read more about us, please consider allowing us to welcome the child you are carrying into our family, and our strong circle of love.**

What's with the Bold and Italics?

Elicia and I both have a lot to say to you, and we wanted to find a way for you to hear both our voices in this letter. *We thought it would be fun to use italics when I (Elicia) am speaking,* and regular type when it's me (Nelson). *A lot of times, we want to say the exact same thing,* so when it appears in black bold type, we're both speaking together.

Why we want to Adopt

We've always wanted a family, always wanted to be able to share in the miracle of life and the closeness only a family can have. Elicia's so caring, and has such a big heart. *And Nelson's just so great with kids. They love him, tussling and playing about. He can't get enough of them.* **Our arms are big hugs waiting to happen.**

So when we discovered we couldn't have children, we realized that adopting a child, welcoming a new life into our family, would be a great blessing to us. *We long to rock a child in our arms and comfort them with our heartbeats. We want all the runny noses, the tears, the shrieks of joy, and the endless questions.* We're happily looking to adoption as the way to begin our family. We have a lot to offer a child throughout the stages of their life.

We want to be a Mom and Dad.

Raising a Child

Nelson and I both had excellent educations, and our children will, too. It's always been the most important thing in my family. Education creates opportunities. In fact, although we haven't been able to have children (we've tried for five years), both Elicia and I have been active in a mentor program that helps disadvantaged kids get through high school and into college. *Nelson's student, Lisandro, just graduated from high school and is going to be the first in his family to go to college.* I'm really proud of him.

Being mentors has given us a taste of how involved we need to be in our children's education. It's so much more than "how was school today?" We will join them in learning all about this world, and share their joy of discovery. We both read constantly, and can't wait to read to our children all the bedtime stories we grew up with.

We both traveled and saw a lot of the world when we were young. Our children will, too. We feel it is so important that a child see how differently people live around the world. *Some of these wonderful differences can also be found in our own back yard, the city of Los Angeles. A child here can experience the cultures of people from Mexico, China, Japan, India, Thailand, Israel, and Africa without traveling at all.*

We believe that every child is unique and special, and want to provide the individual love, nurturing, and support they need to grow, thrive, and be who they are. Though I suspect that Elicia will spoil them rotten. *I will not! Ahhhhh... All right, I confess. It's probably true. I'm an only child and my parents spoiled me with love.* As I was saying, I think kids also need constancy and routine in their lives, some creative discipline, and to learn responsibility for themselves and others. I think you can give a child that within a supportive environment. *I agree.*

Our Home

We live in a great neighborhood, quiet and hilly, with a park and recreation center near the lake at the bottom of the hill. *It's residential and safe, away from the craziness of the city. We also have one of the best elementary schools in the district.*

We own our home, a sweet little three bedroom, Spanish-style house. Elicia planted and tends our beautiful garden. *When we moved in, the place needed work. Nelson almost single-handedly remodeled the kitchen and downstairs. He's really good with tools.* We're both originally from New York, but have become addicted to the sunshine and warm climate in Los Angeles.

Mealtimes are special to us. We can both cook up a storm, and we take turns making delicious things. *I love that he's as good a cook as I am.* We look forward to dinner together. *Sometimes we sit in the dining room, and talk about the day, share our thoughts, or make plans for the weekend. Sometimes we watch TV, especially, it seems, during basketball season.* So sue me, I love the Lakers.

On weekends, we go out and play, or shop, or sometimes just putter in the garden. You should smell Elicia's roses! *On Sunday, I sing in the choir at church.* I was raised in the Jewish religion. A spiritual life has always been important to us, although we haven't always been involved in organized religious practice. **Both of us feel that a child needs a moral and ethical education as well as an academic one.** *We're planning on exposing our children to the rich cultural traditions of both of our faiths.*

Work

Like most families today, Elicia and I both work. It allows us to live a comfortable life, own our own home, and provide a better future for our family. *I've found a profession I really enjoy, and I think it sets a good example for a child to see their mother fulfilled by what she does. Women are a vital part of society.*

And her work situation is ideal for raising children. *That's true. I work in a big old converted mansion, on a hilltop acre of land overlooking the city. We're a small company that makes television commercials, and we have on-site day care. It's great. The kids come* upstairs and visit us throughout the day, and sit with us at lunch. Everyone loves them; they get so much attention. *I'll be able to see the baby throughout the day whenever I feel the urge.* **In fact, Elicia's bosses both have adopted children.**

I'm a freelance writer and I work out of a home office, which is ten feet down the hall from the baby's room. I write articles for magazines on a variety of subjects, like home remodeling, golf, and the internet. I also have a couple of books in the works. *Many of our friends are creative people, too-artists, designers, actors, filmmakers, and writers.* Our children will grow up in a creative and stimulating environment.

The great thing about our careers is that they will allow our children to grow up with the active involvement of both parents. Elicia will take them to work some days, and I will play with them at home on others. Our children will get lots of attention from the both of us. *Together, we make a good income that makes us comfortably upper middle class. It's important to us that we provide the best possible opportunities for our children.*

Our Hobbies and Interests

We relish our playtime, and can't wait to have children with which to share it. We live by the beach, and both love to swim. *We both golf,* although I admit I'm the more addicted of the two. *Addicted puts it mildly.* We also love to scuba dive, which Elicia taught me to do shortly after we met. *He's like a fish when he's in the water.*

We like to be outside, and California is a great place to live. *We're in excellent health and we plan to stay that way.* If you've got your health, you've got everything. We're both 40, but young for our age. *We garden, take hikes, go to the beach, and ride bikes. One of our ideal vacations is the surf-and-turf special where we can scuba dive and play golf, preferably on a warm island.* I can't wait to teach the kids to swim.

Elicia sings like a bird. She's got a beautiful voice and our house is full of music. *I'm blushing.* It's true. *When I was growing up, my parents always encouraged me to pursue the activities that brought me happiness. I discovered my love of singing and performing all on my own. I joined my first church when I was seven because my friends were in the youth choir.*

The Family

Well, Elicia is an only child, so Bob and Geri can't wait to become Grandma & Grandpa. *If you think they spoiled me rotten...* I know, we're going to have to hold them back forcibly. *His mother is no better.* Elicia's got me there. My mom lives nearby, so I'm sure her grandchild will be overwhelmed with love and attention. I also have two sisters, one of whom is local. My father passed away.

Though I'm an only, I have a huge extended family, mostly in North Carolina. My grandmother, who's 89 years old, was one of ten children. When we went back east for the family reunion, they rented the social hall of the church in order to hold everybody. *There're a lot of them.* **We'd like to adopt a second child as well, so they'll both grow up with siblings.**

In addition to our families, we have a large and close circle of friends, many of them with young children. *Marcel and David, our friends next door, are expecting, so the babies will grow up together. Our best friend Rose lives two doors down. She has no children, but can't wait to be an Aunt.* Our neighborhood is like our extended family.

Elicia was married once before; she's my one and only. *I got married way too young the first time. It only lasted a couple of years. I needed to grow up and discover who I was. When I met Nelson, in my late twenties, I was ready to build a life with him.* Even then, she had to be sure. We spent 5 years together before we got married. *We've been married 6 years now and our relationship just gets better and better.* I second that emotion

We're best friends, as well as husband and wife.

In Conclusion...

You are a very brave young woman to be bringing a new life into the world under uncertain circumstances. *We know this is a difficult time in your life, but we think that it can be a positive one as well. By sharing it with you, we can give you confidence that the child you are bearing will be welcome with open arms into a loving family.*

We hope that we can go on this journey with you, and turn this miracle of life into a time of joy for us all.

Thanks for reading this, and take care, Nelson & Elicia

APPENDIX 3:
ADDITIONAL SAMPLE LETTERS

Here are a number of letters in a variety of styles. I selected them because, although they are each vastly different from one another, each seems quite genuine and authentic. Each gives the feeling that you have spent some time with these people and really learned something salient about them.

For more examples, some good, some bad, visit the Dear Birthmother letter registry at Adoption.com and browse through the many letters there, or ask your adoption professional for samples. Reading many letters teaches you what works and what doesn't.

He Says/ She Says

Here's a lovely example of the He says/She says form. It's full of respect and enthusiasm. This couple could have illustrated their points with more, specific, examples, but overall, they do an excellent job of shining through the text. Their subheads are common for this form.

Dear Birth Mom,

Hi. Our names are Heide and Jacob and we want to thank you for reading our letter. We hope that we can make a very difficult time for you just a little bit less so by telling you a bit about ourselves and our commitment to raising a child in our loving family. Although we can't begin to know the journey that has brought you to us, we do know you must be caring and selfless, because you are considering adoption out of the greatest love for your child.

About Us

We recently celebrated our 4th anniversary, but we met while volunteering two years before that. We quickly became best friends, and we built a deeply loving marriage upon respect, honesty, and trust. After three years of infertility, we are so excited and ready to adopt! We have so much love to give and are eager to nurture your baby and provide him or her with all the wonderful opportunities the world has to offer.

Our warm three-story townhouse in Chicago is always filled with family and friends. The beautiful tree-lined street and neighborhood is a great place for kids. Living just a block from Lake Michigan with its endless parks and playgrounds is a real treat!

We spend most of our free time together. In the warm weather, we love to grill and garden. We often take walks to our friends' houses, grab a sweet treat, or a glance through the book-

store. But when we're home, we love to snuggle up with a good book or game, or a movie. We look forward to endless bedtime stories and an epic family Monopoly tournament. On weekends, we love to try new restaurants, see movies, or go to the theater. We've traveled a lot together, but we really can't wait to take trips as a family!

About Heide:

I grew up in the suburbs of Atlanta, and currently work for a wonderful businessman, distributing his donations to local charities (basically, I get to give away somebody else's money!). I can't wait to be a stay-at-home mom. In my free time, I love to cook Italian food, entertain for our wonderful friends, and volunteer at the local women's clinic.

Jacob and I both come from very close families. Almost all of my extended family still lives in Chicago, which allows us to see each other all the time and spend all of the holidays together. I am extremely close to my three younger sisters. Growing up, we were constantly together and not a day goes by that I do not talk to them on the phone or by e-mail.

My parents instilled in me a strong emphasis on helping others, being a kind person, and getting the best education possible. Jacob and I want to pass on these values to our children. My parents are extremely excited to become grandparents and to spoil their first grandchild with love and kisses.

I want to tell you about Jacob: I fell in love with Jacob almost immediately. He is the most thoughtful, honest, smart and loyal person that I have ever known. And when he smiles and laughs his whole face lights up. He is always there to help me, my family, or even someone he doesn't know. Most of all, I love seeing *the joy on Jacob's face when he plays with our nieces, teaches them new songs, or feeds our friend's new baby. I love him very much, and I can't wait to see him caring for our child!*

About Jacob*:*

I grew up in a suburb of Chicago. After college, I earned my law degree, and have worked at the same law firm since graduation. Like Heide, I too am lucky to have a close family. Actually, my parents, grandma and sister (with her family) all live in the same Chicago suburb. This makes it easy for my parents to spend lots of time with their grandchildren. And when we have our children, you can guess where they want us to move.

We are very close with my sister and her family and I am particularly happy that she and Heide are not just sisters-in-law, but virtually sisters. Our adorable nieces, Brenna and Naomi (5&3), are the lights in our life. And, even at a young age, they can't wait for a new cousin. Since they often spend the weekend with us, we have more toys in our home than any childless couple we know.

I would like to tell you about Heide: *I fell in love with Heide because she has the biggest heart of anyone I have ever met. Her caring nature is probably why children love her so much. They know that she truly wants the best for them. Heide is also incredibly thoughtful. No special occasion of a friend or family member goes by without a gift from her (and from me, but only because she signs my name to the card). Heide has a wonderfully warm and fun-loving personality and I love to hang out with her. She will be an amazing mom!*

We Love Kids:

Simply put, we want to adopt because we love kids. Heide always babysits for our nieces and nephews, and our neighborhood knows her as the person to call if parents need help in a pinch. Likewise, Jacob loves to play and care for children (and they love to play with him!) ***As parents, we promise to love your baby unconditionally, with support and guidance.***

Thank you again for taking the time to read our letter. We want you to know that if you choose to place your baby with us we will always be fully aware of the magnitude of the blessing you have given us and thankful for letting us be good parents to your child. We want to welcome you into our lives, and we hope you will want to get to know us better as we have much more to share with you. ***Feel free to call us toll free at …***

Subject

Here's another great letter, organized by subject, but also incorporating some he says/she says writing. It's full of active verbs, energy, and enthusiasm. It employs very creative subheads and gives you a strong sense of the authors' character. This letter distinguishes itself by the strength and clarity of its voice.

Welcome To Our Garden!

We are Carole and Stan and we are so excited to share ourselves with you. First, we want to thank you. We know that your adoption plan represents most profound acts of love imaginable. As adoptive parents, we will always be dedicated to honor-

ing and continuing that love. We will ensure that our child grows to understand and respect your courage and selflessness. We hope this letter conveys this to you. If it does, and you like what you see, maybe we can unite to welcome and nurture a new soul into our wonderful, whimsical world. Most importantly, we hope to be a positive part of your experience, whether you select us or not.

The Seeds Are Planted (A Little Background)

From Carole: Stan is 35 and originally from Wisconsin. He was a high school athlete and one of those kids who got into trouble for talking too much in class. He made up for it by being an extremely good student in college and law school. Now he's a lawyer and part-owner of an insurance agency. I love him more every day. He's the funniest, most truthful and sincere man I've ever met. His insight, wisdom, and tenderness will make him an amazing father.

From Stan: Carole is 29 years old and hails from Tennessee. She has two wonderful sisters and a large close knit family. In high school, she played tennis, basketball and ran track. In college she majored in marketing and ran cross-country. Later, she acquired a degree in early childhood education and began working as a preschool teacher. She loves her job because it provides her the opportunity to nurture children and share in their growth. When we become parents, however, she plans to become a stay-at-home mom so she can focus on our child.

But these fine qualities and accomplishments don't really capture the essence of my wife. Carole's a woman of uncompromising integrity, unyielding compassion, enduring patience, and a magical way with people. She volunteers with young children and the elderly, and you've never seen someone create so many smiles. She is tender but disciplined, strong or soft, as the occasion requires. I am one of the luckiest men in the world to be able to start a family with her, and I can't wait to share that luck with a child.

Sunshine in Our Garden (Getting Married and Ready for Kids)

Love gave us a beautiful canvas on which to paint our lives. We fell in love in 1995 and got married on June 21, 1996, the summer solstice and the longest day of the year. We picked that day because we want our marriage to last as long as the light. We've been planning on starting a family ever since.

Soon after, we bought our dream home, a magical old house that was built in 1918 in a charming residential area of Boston. The streets are lined with tall trees and there are several parks nearby. Kids surround us in the neighborhood, and we've often imagined them playing in our yard with children of our own. We also enjoy fishing and swimming at our family cabin on a lake in New Hampshire. We have two dogs, George and Gracie, who are wonderful with children, and pretty fair swimmers themselves.

Tending the Family Garden

When we think about being parents, we think about passing on the unconditional love and stability that our families provided us. We trust that this foundation, coupled with the happy way we live, will help instill in our children a strong sense of integrity and compassion. We wish to raise children who celebrate their spirituality, hold fast to their own moral philosophies, and relish the small beauties of life. We want them to have fun while understanding that life can be a demanding learning process. We also want them to know that hard work can be fulfilling.

What does all this mean on a daily level? We want our children to have fun positive experiences. As babies, they'll have toys and games that challenge them physically and mentally in a warm, safe environment. We will encourage them to be creative and work with others. We will expose them to all types of music, books, and sports. We'll teach them to play ball and swim. We'll do chores together, too. We'll take out the trash and mow the lawn. We'll wash the dogs. We'll sing. We'll eat ice cream and cake. We'll celebrate holidays.

We can't wait to introduce our children to all that life has to offer, from its grand views to its subtle details, from its intricate complexities to its simple truths. We'll travel to faraway places together and learn about other cultures. We will read to them and stress the importance of communication. We'll provide the opportunity for a first rate education.

As they grow, we'll go to church together and volunteer together. We'll teach them to cook healthy food and we'll eat together. We'll support them when they struggle, applaud them when they do well and guide them when they make mistakes. We will love them every day.

We will provide the canvas and brushes so they can paint their lives. We will offer them all we have and know. Then we'll watch them paint. Nobody can predict the outcome. That exciting mystery makes it all worthwhile. But God willing, we will marvel at their work.

Wanna Grow Our Gardens Together?

We also understand that being the best parents we can be may include helping you during your pregnancy. We care about you. We will financially assist you with your pregnancy-related

*needs to the extent permitted by law. After the birth, we are
willing to stay as close or distant as you want. We could exchange
information through letters, pictures, or third parties. We all
share a common goal, the happiness of your child, and wish you
all the best.*

*So now, the next move is up to you. You probably have a lot
of thinking to do. We wish there was more we could do to help
you in this process. If our letter makes you think that we might be
a good match, just let us know. We'd love to speak with you on the
phone, or meet if you'd like. We also have an album with lots
more pictures we could mail to you. We look forward to hearing
from you.*

With respect and affection, Stan & Carole

Blended Voice/Reporter

Dear Birth Parents,

*Thank you for having the courage and love to place your
child for adoption. We appreciate the care that you are taking to
select a family that will give your baby all that you wish for them.
We want you to know that there is nothing that we want more in
our life than to share it with a son or daughter, and we eagerly
anticipate sharing the joy and love in our lives with a child.*

*We first fell in love in 1994, but the happiest day of our lives
was July 19, 1997, the day we got married at St. Dominic's
church. We planned the wedding together. It had an herbal theme
and the fragrant scent of lavender and rosemary filled the church
as we walked down the aisle. Patrick's family and best friend flew
in from New Jersey for the bachelor party, rehearsal, and wed-*

ding. The dance of our life together began with a beautiful jazz quartet that sent us into the evening. It was a magnificent time in our lives that we shall always delight in sharing with our child through pictures, videos, and stories.

Maggie has worked at a large botanical garden. She delights in thrilling children to the explosion of colors and scents of a rose garden in springtime. The garden is a pleasurable place to go bird watching and to feed the koi fish that live in the ponds, and in the summer, we love to go to the music concerts and outdoor theater. She has also found her bliss teaching kids about vegetables and herbs as they plant their own gardens. Maggie now stays at home to prepare our own garden to educate and delight our child with herbs, flowers, and vegetables. In the spring and summer, she always fills the house with flowers. We can't wait to share these joys with our child.

Patrick works in sales, where he teaches a group of 25 agents the art of sales. He has been very successful, mostly because people trust him right away. He's close with his co-workers, many of whom have small children. Company picnics are really fun since there are lots of little kids running around and playing. Our children will get to play with kids from a variety of cultures and backgrounds.

We delight in our time together outside of work. We take day trips to Manhattan Beach or weekend trips along the California coastline. Sometimes we just go out to dinner and a movie. Whatever we are doing, we relish each other's company and the time we spend together. We look forward to sharing our adventures with a youngster and creating new ones as a family.

We've both traveled extensively. It's a passion with us, and we can't wait to expose our child to the excitement and education of visiting foreign places. Our future plans include trips to Ireland and Scotland, where Patrick has family.

Maggie loves to read. She loves visiting the library and browsing bookstores. We both have a strong appreciation of the arts—music, art, literature, and dance—and we'll introduce our child to the wonderful opportunities for self-expression they can bring. One of Patrick's favorite pastimes is golf. He shares this hobby with his mother and father, who are already checking into Fisher-Price's line of toy golf clubs for the baby. Patrick also loves watching sports and looks forward to teaching our child to root for the New York and Catholic teams.

Our spirituality plays an important role in our lives. Although Patrick is Catholic and Maggie is a Religious Scientist, we both respect each other's beliefs and often attend services together, which we will continue to do as a family. Our beliefs have so much in common and the differences make for some spirited discussions.

Patrick's parents live one block from the Atlantic Ocean in a summer resort town. We visit every Christmas and often in the summer. These vacations give us a chance to spend time with Patrick's family, including his 97-year-old grandmother. Maggie's family lives nearby and plans to spend lots of time with the baby. Maggie's sister is also a Doula, and she works with mothers and their infants to help them make the transition into a new life together. Both of our families can't wait to smother our child with affection.

Our cats, Scooter, Katerie, and Dorian Grey, have always treated us well and we have appreciated the kindness that they have shown by allowing us into their home. After a long family meeting, they have given their approval to the addition of a new *family member. However, Scooter called first dibs on fetch, Katerie insists on grooming rights, and Dorian just wants to look.*

We realize that you have a difficult decision and we respect the time that you are taking to make it. Know that our child will always understand the love and consideration you gave to their adoption plan. Our home is filled with love, joy and support and we can't wait to welcome a new life into it. We appreciate you considering us to be the parents of your child.

Peace and Love, Maggie and Patrick

Guest Narrator

Bonjour! I'm Jean-Paul (they also call me Pépé) and I'm a year and half old. I'm writing this letter (true, Maurice and Regine, my parents are helping just a little bit) to tell you about our world and to say how much we would like to adopt your baby. I swear, I will be the best big brother in the whole wide world!

Dad and Mom met over ten years ago at an artsy-fartsy party and haven't been alone since. After ten years of marriage, they still love each other lots and lots, and have tons of fun together.

There is nothing traditional or usual about them, let me tell you. Dad is a director in the movie business and Mom is a writer. She is writing a book just for me and my future brother or sister. They like books and movies, gardens and the ocean. Mom loves growing roses and Dad loves to surf (I will someday, too). They both love to sail and look at the stars on a clear, summer night.

They adopted me last year and so they know all about

adoption (there is a whole shelf full of adoption books in the living room!) They even drove five hundred miles in the middle of the night to see me born. We recently wrote a letter to my birth mom, and we send her pictures and keep in contact, it's really nice. She's very excited that I'm going to be a big brother.

Mom (Maman, in French) is from France. Mom met Dad on her first trip to America when she was working as a curator in a contemporary art museum in Germany. She didn't even speak English. I think they liked each other so much because they couldn't understand a word that the other said. She is a super cook (I had all my baby food homemade) and we always try all kinds of different food. She's a great Mom and she loves us both so much you would forget that her family actually eats frog's legs and snails!

Dad (Papa is the Frenchy way to say it) has a degree in film from some school in California (even though he was born in New York) and he tells people what to do all day long. He gets to decide when and where he wants to work and that's really cool. Sometimes Mom and I get to visit him on the set where he's usually pointing to things and everybody is running around doing what he says. Somehow, they pay him for doing this.

He has a sister and Mom in New York and extended family in Maine. Dad likes to go snowboarding (plus that surfing stuff) and we like to wrestle on the couch too. Sometimes we play airplane until he gets tired. We also like to go camping in the desert and river rafting. He reads me bedtime stories, and he says that soon we will make paintings with wet potatoes in his favorite color, bright orange.

We live in a big house in a quiet part of town in Texas with a super big yard; I can't even see the front part when we're standing at the back part! We have lots of modern furniture, which the dogs and I love to scratch, and there is also some strange stuff called art on the walls (I am not sure why, but you are not supposed to touch it.) There's lots of sun where we live and lots of birds and stuff.

In the summer, we go swimming in a nearby lake. We have barbecues with all our friends and watch the sunset while sipping Mom's homemade limeade, which is real tasty. Maman makes some French pancakes called crepes, but the French eat them for desert, not for breakfast, I eat them for both of course, and I eat so many I think I'm gonna pop!

We get to travel a lot. Besides France, I've been to Mexico and the Bahamas and Germany and Switzerland. We've also visited Dad's family in New York City. My Grandie is there and she teaches me how to dance and plays pat-a-cake with me. She's also a pastry chef so there's no end to the sweet things to eat. We visited France last Christmas to see Mom's family, they're really nice (oui, oui!)) and I got to see all my cousins and aunts and uncles and grandparents and well, you get the idea. A bunch of the family lives in Switzerland and Dad says that we will go skiing there when I get older.

Me, I just like to play with the dogs, Zoom-Babe and Zapata, who I ride like a horse. My parents tell everybody that I am a great kid, very sociable and very easygoing. I like music and books and toys.

So, we have a great life, we love each other a whole bunch but something is missing. We all want me to be a big brother but Mom and Dad say it isn't so easy. When we were in France there was this big church, and on top of it, they had carved a stork in stone. I thought storks are where babies came from but Mom and

Dad said no, babies come from people who are really special, people with the biggest hearts in the whole world, and one day, one of these special people will give us another baby to take care of. They will have so much love that they even have enough for us too.

Ok, that's all for today, thank you for looking at Mom and Dad, don't forget to call them! I think they are super parents, and will be, too, for the baby inside you. I promise they will be the best!

Love,

Jean-Paul, the small one

This next letter is also written in the voice of a young child, but is full of lovely details and telling behaviors that give you a strong sense of this couple as parents.

Hi!

My name is Stanley and I want to be a big brother. My parents and I want another baby, but we need your help. Let me tell you some of the great things about us and you will see why we might be the right family for your baby.

Mommy and Daddy have been married for 12 years, and they were friends for 5 years before that. They love being together and really enjoy one another's company. They are each other's best friends. Mommy and Daddy make a pretty good team, too! They make all of our household decisions together, like who will stay at home to take care of me, and they support each other even when they don't agree.

Mommy's name is Sally, and she's a third grade teacher at a nearby school. I like to visit her there, and when I'm bigger, I'll go to that school, too! Mom likes to read, sew, and work in the garden. She never remembers the punchline to a joke, is crazy about Winnie the Pooh, and is totally addicted to chocolate. She sings to me and plays with me. We go for walks together, or take a ride in my red wagon (she gets in sometimes, too). I especially love when she reads to me, because she makes up a different voice for every character in the story.

My daddy's name is Andy. He used to be a restaurant manager, but now he stays home full time to take care of me. He's a funny guy who's just a big kid at heart. He likes all types of music, and tends to break into song for no particular reason. He loves to take photos (especially of me), and he cooks a mean tuna-noodle casserole. We like to go to the zoo together, and he's introducing me to some pretty big bones at the Natural History museum. Sometimes we just sit and cuddle or play with my toys, but I really like it when he plays "tickle monster" and chases me around the house!

You've already met me. I'm Stanley. I'm 3 years old. I love to laugh and play. I especially love my Hot Wheels cars and I am crazy about ELMO! I am usually a happy guy, and I am very friendly. I really look forward to having a little brother or sister to play with. I know together we will laugh a lot, get into trouble a little, tell many secrets, and be lifelong friends. I was adopted, too, so I know all about where babies come from. They are a blessing to mommies and daddies from special people who love their child enough to want the best for them. Although my birthmother lives in another state, we call her and send her letters with pictures so she knows how I'm doing. I love to hear from her and know she is thinking of me, too.

We live in a nice neighborhood within walking distance of open farmland, parks, family and friends and school. We own our own home, which has three bedrooms, two bathrooms, and room enough to play. I have a Golden Retriever named Sigmund who is my good friend, and a bunny named Sylvia who lives most of the time at my mommy's school, but comes home on weekends to play with me.

My family is pretty great, and as you can see, we have a lot of love to give. I hope you will consider us when you decide to place your baby for adoption.

Ten Things...

10 Things You'll Want to Know about Phillis and Sam

1. We're committed to an Open Adoption.

We hope to have a "life long connection" with you. This includes letters, pictures, visits, etc. We believe open adoption empowers everyone involved, and we hope you feel that way too.

2. Phyllis will be a stay-at-home mom.

I was a nurse, but I want nothing more than to devote myself to providing a child with a stable home, chock full of love, attention, fun and daily adventures. Sam works as an accountant, but he plans to be home every night at 5:00 to spend lots of time with the baby.

3. Your child will be our first child.

But we'd love to adopt a second so that they can have some sibling fun. Both of us come from large families, and every year we join our brothers and sisters, and all their children (13 in all!) at our parents' house to celebrate a big Christmas morning. The kids all dress as elves and hand out the presents.

4. Your child will have the security and unconditional love of two parents.

We've always viewed being parents as the next big journey in our lives. We've tried to have a baby since we were married 6 years ago (together for 4 before that!). If possible, our struggles with infertility have made our love that much stronger and our communication that much deeper. We're best friends as well as husband and wife, and can't wait to welcome a baby into our lives.

5. We sincerely respect you and care about your situation.

We want to surround you with understanding people who support your decision and can offer you any resources that may be helpful. We know that pregnancy presents new challenges and we're committed to making yours as healthy and happy as we can.

6. Our spacious house is in a terrific family-oriented neighborhood that is filled with kids.

The backyard has trees to climb and a hill perfect for summersaults in summer and sledding in winter. Phyllis surrounds us with flowers, and I've already drawn up plans to build the safest tree house ever made. I've always dreamed of camping out overnight in the back yard with my children and showing them all the constellations in the sky.

7. We are financially secure.

Sam is a Senior Vice President at his company. We have resources for trips to Disney World and for a college education, if that is what our child wishes (though we believe college provides *the best leg up a person can have).*

8. We value many things such as family, friendship, compassion, honesty, faith, hard work, courage, and keeping an open mind.

Though not particularly religious people, we believe that you learn your values at home. We will do our best to see that our child gains a moral and ethical foothold in the world, and grows up to love and respect our common humanity.

9. We know how to have fun!

We're outdoorsy people. Anything you can do under an open sky with the people you love brings us great joy. We took our last vacation to Yosemite, where we camped out, grilled hot dogs on the open fire, and hiked up the river to a beautiful waterfall. The only hitch was when Sam woke up in the middle of the night convinced a bear was stealing our food. After madly tearing up the tent looking for something to protect us with, he took his flashlight and a spatula outside to scare off a big, mean… raccoon! I laughed for days. He's my hero.

10. We would be honored to meet you and would love to hear your dreams for your child.

The adoption triad is made up loving adults united for the good of the child. Your son or daughter will always know the love you carry for him or her, as well as the care you showed in finding the very best home for him or her to grow up in. We know we can provide such a home, and we'd love to meet with you to see if it's the right one for your child.

Thank you very much for reading our "10 things." We wish you the very best!

h 6/12 P